a time for change?

REVISIONING YOUR CALL

James E. Hightower, Jr. and
W. Craig Gilliam

Foreword by Richard N. Bolles
Author of *What Color Is Your Parachute?*

Library of Congress Catalog Card Number 00-104840
ISBN 1-56699-233-8

CONTENTS

When professional ministers wrestle with the issue of whether to stay where they are—or not, or whether to stay in professional ministry—or not, most of them want some help with their decision. Every minister, priest, or rabbi who is wrestling with the issue of transition or career change will find helpful companionship in this book by James Hightower and Craig Gilliam.

A variety of help is available out there, and generally it falls into the following categories:

1. *Help from within ourselves*, and from the Spirit, often encountered through a process of writing about ourselves in a journal. It is often amazing what you learn about yourself when you try to talk to yourself. The process itself can pull forth stunning insights. The Holy Spirit has a field day.

2. *Help from a person, face to face.* This person could be a family member or friend, a therapist, pastoral counselor, or spiritual director. This person could also be someone you know who has walked this road before you, and who is willing to share his or her learnings, so you don't have to figure out each step on your own.

3. *Help from a person, through the written word.* That word might take the form of a sermon, article, journal, or book. We can break this category down even further into three strategies:

a. *Help that is essentially psychotherapy or counseling.* The authors call this "bibliotherapy." You might deal with either context or with process. Or you might find a middle way and set up a context within which to view the process you are going through. This bibliotherapy might or might not lead to a career transition. As the authors point out, "Depending on what I seek, it might be that no position will satisfy me. What I very well might need is profound healing, a change of heart, and professional help and time to move to that place of healing."

b. Help that is essentially career development. Following the authors' lead, we might call this second path "biblioguidance." If you decide you do want to pursue a calling outside the ordained ministry, you could use various books to help you assess your skills and interests, and then to discern what fields out there look most attractive to you and best match your skills.

c. Help that is essentially step-by-step job-hunting advice. We might call this "biblioplanning." If you decide to seek a job in a new field, you need to know exactly how you plan a job hunt, what you do first, and what "plan B" you will fall back on if the first one doesn't work. Biblioplanning helps you to deal with the nitty-gritty of job-hunting and addresses such questions as, "When I'm asked a question in a job interview, how long should my answer be?"

With this taxonomy in mind, we can classify a particular career-advice book, and when we do so, we often see that a written work falls into more than one of the above categories. For example, my book, *What Color Is Your Parachute? A Practical Manual for Job-Hunters and Career-Changers,* has for thirty years fallen into categories 3b and 3c, while Hightower and Gilliam's book falls into categories 3a and 3b.

The authors cover 3a especially well. That is, they set *context* well and illuminate *the process* involved in weighing transition. The points they make in this book that I particularly like are (and I paraphrase):

•   None of us at the end of our life should end up exactly where we started, in any life-arena—particularly in our vocational life. The developmental task of midcareer *should be* reevaluation. Weighing a career transition is not only normal and desirable but—when done well—can be a great opportunity for healthy change within and without. "The danger is to know you need this searching and then to fail to do it."

•   The question we need to pose to ourselves in our search is, "Am I running from something, or running toward something?" The key to answering this question is to tell ourselves our own story. When we tell it, we should note particularly whether we tell our story as if we are survivors or as if we were victims. By rewriting our story (if we need to) so that we do not view ourselves as victim, we reinvent ourselves.

• The tools we need for such a reinvention are faith, imagination, and humor. The goal of such reinvention is to help us "to transcend our present self."

• The key to transcending ourselves is to revisit the question of "our calling." Using Richard Niebuhr's description of the four kinds of calling, the authors offer some invigorating questions to ask ourselves. The key point they make for the minister weighing a transition is "making your personal faith and your career in ministry synonymous is dangerous."

• When we set out to reinvent ourselves, or—to put it better—when we set out to allow God to transcend, transform and transfigure us, changes appear that are of such magnitude we call them changes in a system. Hence, we need to have some sophistication and knowledge about how systems—including the systems in which we find ourselves—operate.

In particular, we need to stay aware of the fact that systems (church, family) naturally respond to change by trying to maintain their present condition—to keep their balance, to achieve homeostasis. We also need to understand that the functioning of any one person moving toward change has an affect on all others in that system (family, church). Hence, career upheavals can cause marital upheavals too. The authors emphasize that the question facing every thoughtful minister is, "How can I undergo transition in such a way that it minimizes the negative effect it can have on my family system?" The authors offer a lot of guidance for ministers facing this quandary.

In sum, if you are reevaluating your ministry, looking for guidance, and want a clearer and more fruitful context from which to view what's happening to you and in you; if you are willing to keep a journal and do some writing (or rewriting) of your own story; if you are seeking transformation, you will find this book of Hightower and Gilliam's very helpful.

Richard N. Bolles
Author, *What Color Is Your Parachute?*

A Time for Change? Re-Visioning Your Call is the work of James E. Hightower, Jr., and W. Craig Gilliam. Both are clergy and work for The McFarland Institute in New Orleans, Louisiana. Gilliam is director of The McFarland Center for Clergy and Congregational Care, and Hightower is director of The McFarland Pastoral Counseling Center. This book is designed to serve as a reflective and practical tool to assist clergy who are considering career changes. Jim's and Craig's research sources include:

- The experiences of both, including years of service in the local church as ministers and several career transitions.
- Interviews with clergy from various denominations who are undergoing or have undergone career changes, or have seriously considered the option.
- Professional work with clergy in transition in the authors' roles with the McFarland Institute as consultants and counselors.

Chapters 1 and 3 were written by Craig Gilliam and chapters 2, 4, and 5 by Jim Hightower. Because of the topic and the authors' perspectives, some of the material overlaps, but each author approaches the topic from a somewhat different perspective, offering the reader various experiential resources with which to identify or from which to draw.

Jim and Craig thank God and each person who has played a significant role on their journey. Life has sometimes been challenging, but it has never been boring and has always been a gift. To God and to each of you who have supported Jim and Craig in their work, thank you!

We hope you enjoy this book and find it helpful to you on your journey. May God bless you wherever your path may lead. Shalom!

CHAPTER 1

The Original Vision of Our Call

Interviewing a pastor in the later years of his ministry, I asked, "Have you ever considered changing careers and leaving professional ministry?" He answered, "Any minister who has not seriously considered that at some point is, in my opinion, not worth his or her weight in salt." Through many discussions with ministers I have found that the impulse to pursue another career is an almost universal experience. We have written this book to address the issue of change for clergy who have reached such a place on their journeys. We will reflect with you on healthy questions to consider in exploring paths to follow, offer practical suggestions we have gathered from other ministers who have traveled this road, highlight research on re-envisioning one's call, and share insights from our own experiences of career change.

To lay the groundwork for this book, I emphasize two principles on which we build. First, to entertain the possibility of leaving professional ministry is not to be condemned or viewed as a sign of failure; rather, it should be accepted as part of the spiritual journey. The greatest failure for a minister would be to refuse to hear one's inner voice or attend to one's inner stirring, for the voice might be one's call, and the struggle to interpret it might be the most direct path to vocation. The Old Testament narrative of Jacob offers a model for this struggle.

Jacob's journey brings him to the stream of Jabbok. He discovers that on the other side of the stream is his brother, Esau, who Jacob thinks will kill him. The one from whom Jacob ran, the one who started him on his journey, now stands at the end of the journey waiting to meet him. The night before crossing the stream to see Esau, Jacob sends his wives and maids across the river to his brother's abode. Jacob wants to spend the night alone. Fear drives him into his soul. Unexpectedly, an adversary leaps out of the darkness and wrestles with him. He does not ask for a visit from the stranger, but once this being appears, he has to deal with the challenge. According to the narrative, Jacob wrestles with this stranger all night. When morning begins to dawn, the stranger wants to leave, but Jacob will not let him. Showing his power, the stranger touches Jacob on the hip-socket, and his hip is torn out of the joint. The stranger struggles to get away, but Jacob, though exhausted, refuses to let him go. First the stranger must bless him, Jacob says. Jacob wants to know this dark stranger's name. He will not let the stranger depart until he knows the meaning of this experience. The stranger says, "You shall no longer be called Jacob, but Israel, for you have striven with God and have prevailed" (Genesis 32:22-32). From a psychological perspective, a change of name suggests a change in nature. Jacob has been transformed through the experience. As a result he limps away, different because of his struggles but having grown from them.

Imagine that the urge that surfaces in us to consider a career change is the dark adversary that leaps on us out of the darkness. Like Jacob, we do not consciously choose this urge, but the ominous question surfaces apart from our choosing. It comes from our inner life, our external situation, or a combination of the two. The healthy response is to wrestle with the feeling that has stirred or with the voice that has whispered, as Jacob wrestled through the night. We must ask the adversary's name and meaning and not let it go until it tells us what we seek to know. The struggle will be painful and ominous, and we, like Jacob, will walk away with an unforgettable limp, but we will be changed for the better. Through struggling and wrestling with this dark figure, we may learn that the urge to move away from professional ministry may mean not a forsaking of our call but a movement to another, deeper call of the spirit and soul. Feminist theologian Nelle Morton writes,

> There is not a road ahead. We make the road as we go. The clue of the beginnings is more often not discovered until the end . . . maybe the journey [re-imaging our call] is not so much a journey ahead, but a journey into presence. The greatest journey is to be present with the one nearest to you.[1]

The one to whom we need to be present may be the dark stranger that leaps on us in the night, which may be the call, however it comes and wherever it leads us.

To assess your inner voice, ask yourself the following questions. You may wish to write out your answers.

- What road am I taking? Am I allowing myself to be present with the one, the dark stranger, who might echo my call, who is nearest to me?

- What does the dark stranger who comes in the night represent within me?

- As a minister thinking of leaving professional ministry, how would it feel for me to be present to and wrestle with this stranger who leaps onto me in the night?

- What is the name of the stranger who appears when I am in that frightened state, alone, waiting to confront my adversary?

The first principle we discussed is that thinking of leaving professional ministry is not to be condemned or viewed as a sign of failure; rather it should be accepted as part of the spiritual journey. The second principle is that going into a new career away from the institutional church does not mean that one is leaving the ministry, but rather that one is changing the mode of expressing that ministry. In interviewing clergy who have left professional ministry in the institutional church, I was careful not to phrase their actions as "leaving the ministry." Several ministers whom I interviewed pointed out that they did not leave the ministry, and that they will always be ministers. What they left was the *professional expression* of ministry through the institutional church. The change or transition comes in the work through which one expresses ministry, the venues chosen and paths followed. One minister who no longer serves a local parish goes daily to coffee shops in the area where he lives. He said:

> The coffee shop is my ministry. I have conversations with people I never had when I was a professional minister. My ministry has not ended because I left the professional position in the church. It has broadened and deepened. Even though the transition was frightening, having done it, I've never found myself wanting, and I have grown because of it. It is not for everyone, but for me, it was the right choice, the right path to follow.

This minister's compelling story prompts the question, "Why do ministers leave the professional ministry?" Reasons ministers leave or consider leaving professional ministry are many. Some of the primary reasons we have found are:

- Stress
- Burnout
- Unrealistic expectations
- Leadership changes in congregations
- Clergy betrayal of church values
- Congregational betrayal of the value system of the clergy
- Clergy scapegoated or made the focus of an anxious system
- Personality conflicts between congregation and clergy
- Disillusionment
- Financial needs

- Inability to live in tension between the institution's demands and beliefs and the minister's own conscience and belief system

For these reasons and no doubt others, clergy have begun seeking nontraditional or alternative ministerial roles and careers.

The list above does not exhaust the reasons ministers leave professional ministry; it is a sample that grows out of the authors' research and interviews. Rather than providing an in-depth analysis of these reasons, we will focus on how to consider change in careers in a way that is healthy, methodical, responsible, and empowering.

Before we explore healthy strategies for change, reflect on your feelings about and reasons for considering a career change. You may also wish to write out your responses to the following question.

- What are your reasons for considering a career change?

PROFESSIONAL DISCERNMENT AND ITS PERSONAL ROOTS

We will discuss three types of career change. The first is a move from professional, pastoral ministry in a local church to a position that uses similar gifts and talents. For example, I might find a new career in an institutional setting, as a pastoral counselor or a social worker. I have skills and training in that area. The change means refocusing the skills I use rather than developing new skills and acquiring new training. The second is a move from clergy status to a career totally unrelated and drastically different. For example, the minister of a parish might decide to become a rocket scientist. That means starting over: Schooling or professional training, time, and money will have to be considered. The third form is departure from a position in ministry without taking another post, at least for a while. This is the most radical option, and few choose this path; nevertheless, it is a decision some make or must confront. For example, some ministers are forced into accepting such a situation when they are terminated. Others might choose this path if they are experiencing burnout or a severe personal or family crisis.

Throughout this book as we explore the topic of career change, be aware of these options. For now, however, we suggest that you ask yourself:

- Which category of career change seems most attractive to me as I consider leaving professional ministry?

For What Are We Searching?

I was with a group of clergy one evening on a retreat, when the moon was full and the stars were glistening. We were discussing Luke 15—the lost coin, the lost sheep, and the lost son. After we had discussed the parables and the images they called up, I asked: "What is represented by the lost sheep, the lost coin, and the lost son in the parables? What do the lost sheep, coin, and son represent for us in our inner lives? More specifically, what is it that we as ministers have lost, and what search brought us into this vocation in the first place?" The room was silent. The questions had stirred the emotions. The dark stranger had jumped out to wrestle with us.

Several ministers and professional counselors I interviewed said that people enter the professional ministry for many reasons, and that motives may be conscious or unconscious. A common theme for people choosing the professional ministry is a search for approval and acceptance. Several clergy noted that a primary reason they entered the ministry was to find the paternal or parental approval and acceptance they had never experienced in their family of origin. (By "family of origin" I mean our biological family; that is, our parents and siblings.) They were looking to the church to give what they felt the family of origin had not given them. Family-of-origin work (an aspect of family systems therapy) is important for ministers if they are to keep these symptoms from recycling. Becoming conscious of their motives and family issues need not cause ministers to renounce their calling, but by becoming aware, they may find clarity about their calling and the nature of their search.

One minister said that what he was searching for, as he moved deeply into his struggle, was to find a home within himself. His constant movement and search were an attempt to accept himself and, in theologian Paul Tillich's language, to "simply accept the fact that you are accepted."[2] As long as he was expecting the church or some other institution or person to "fix" his lack of "at-homeness," the desperate search continued. His statement reminds me of an observation by Presbyterian minister and novelist Frederick Buechner, writing in context of the human journey and not specifically about the journey of the professional minister struggling with vocation:

> To think about home eventually leads you to think back to your childhood home, the place where your life started, the place which off and on throughout your life you keep going back to, if only in dreams and memories, and which is apt to determine the kind of place, perhaps a place inside yourself, that you spend the rest of your life searching for even if you are not aware that you are searching.[3]

Ministry can be a search for the home within ourselves that we have never found and for which we keep searching. One minister put this lack of "at-homeness" in another context when he commented, "Too many ministers enter the ministry looking for love [or] acceptance, or needing love, to the point they cannot give love." In projecting the search to find a home within ourselves onto institutions, situations, or other people, we continue to search outside ourselves for that which we can find only within us.

To illustrate the issue of clergy career change and the unconscious search, I offer an example from my own life. I have undergone the struggle of career change in its most radical form, and I took this path by choice. That experience is the wellspring from which I draw some of the material in this book. I was senior minister of a large congregation. In the parish, things were going well. Then a dark figure unexpectedly leaped out at me, and I began to question my call and place. After a struggle, I chose to leave the church to explore my calling, my vocation. With a wife and small children, I moved to New Orleans. We left a ministry that was going well to move to "no position," but it was our choice. I did not know where the journey was leading, but I knew that the position I left was not where I needed to be.

After our move to New Orleans, I enrolled in school and began searching for employment. My first job was waiting on tables in a prestigious New

Orleans restaurant in the French Quarter. Believe me, sitting at the tables had far more prestige than waiting on them. The move from small-town celebrity to waiter in the French Quarter was an adjustment for my ego. I remember thinking, I hope nobody sees me in this role as a waiter. I had never known how dependent I had become on people's affirmation. I was too dependent. As an inexperienced waiter at the bottom of the restaurant's hierarchy of employees, I began to realize the way life looked from the bottom up rather than from the top down as a senior minister to whom many looked for guidance in a large, aristocratic church in a small community.

After completing my studies, I was offered a position as a professional educator at a local institution. In time, after much prayer and struggle over my calling, my journey brought me where I needed to be. I decided to return to professional ministry, changed denominations, and through the painful process of change became a better minister. Now I am pastor of a small United Methodist parish, as well as director of The McFarland Center for Clergy and Congregational Care in New Orleans, assisting congregations and clergy undergoing change and other challenges.

As I look back, I realize that I did not have to leave any of the ministries I chose to leave, for all were going well. But something in me was unsettled. Finally, the question hit me: "For what am I searching?" I went into therapy with a Jungian analyst to explore this question; through that process, I found that what I was looking for and fleeing from was within me. As a result of the therapeutic process, my spirit grew, my soul deepened, and what I was unconsciously driven by became conscious. I too, like many ministers I interviewed, was looking for affirmation, love, and acceptance. I was looking to the institution to give me what I could find only within myself and God. My experience illustrates the powerful role of the unconscious search in career change, but it also hints at lost innocence or disillusionment, which can also play a role in that change.

The following example demonstrates the lost innocence for which ministers sometimes search. One day, a minister came into my office lamenting his plight. When he was in seminary, he said, he imagined what ministry would be like. When he was appointed to his first church, a difficult appointment, the task was far different from his expectations. In church ministry, he said, much of his work was administration, conflict resolution, and the handling of complaints about insignificant issues. He was tired and disillusioned. This was not, he thought, what ministry was supposed to be.

His expectations differed from his experience. As we discussed his emotional and spiritual frustration, he finally admitted that although this was not what he had expected of ministry, his work in the church was indeed ministry. His innocence about ministry in the local church was lost; the church was what it was, conflict and all. It was like a love relationship when the reality of the first years corrects the projections the lovers had placed on each other. He realized that his disillusionment about ministry in the church had shattered his illusions. This was a necessary process for his maturity in ministry. His question was "Can I live and work in a less-than-perfect institution, an institution that falls short of my expectations?" He came in looking for his lost innocence, his lost illusions about ministry, and left finding something deeper—the acceptance of the loss, which leads to more authentic, mature ministry.

The question "For what am I searching?" is a powerful one for ministers considering a career change. Exploring that question helped me to discern the direction of my journey. Several ministers I interviewed were open to this question, while others found it too threatening to wrestle with. Perhaps that is because the topic touches on core issues of identity.

The question "What have we lost?" is another part of the image in Luke 15 on which we can reflect. Over the years of growth, what have we lost? In what ways do the lost coin, the lost sheep, and the lost son represent something in us for which we search? The question circles around the theological premise that we are called to be whole and complete, as God is. Growing into adulthood, we discover previously unknown parts of ourselves, while losing other aspects. Part of that for which we search was lost along the journey into adulthood. The church father St. Gregory called these lost parts an aspect of our souls for which we search.

Relating to the world outside ourselves offers us insight into our own inner search for wholeness. For example, the homeless represent not only those around us but also someone deep within us who is wandering, hungry, feeling as if he or she does not belong. Those in prison represent that which is caught or caged within us, in the dark, lost, longing to be freed. Maybe we have lost our inner child, whose humor and playfulness we need to rediscover to sustain a healthy life and a deeper connection to others. Thus the journey without is a journey within. That which we seek in the world may represent what we have lost within. What have we lost, and for what are we searching? The lost sheep, the lost coin, and the lost son all represent something we have lost that keeps us from being whole and complete.

The journey is like the woman searching for the lost coin, or the shepherd searching for the lost sheep, or the father waiting and watching for the lost son. We too are searching for that which we have lost—a part of our souls that keeps us from being complete or whole.

"What have we lost and for what are we searching?" is an important question to reflect on as one considers the transition from professional ministry to another career. Before examining your motivations for seeking change or for not changing, reflect on the following questions.

- What have I lost, and for what am I searching?

- Is my search a journey toward home within myself, as Buechner describes it?

- Am I dealing with disillusionment because the disillusionment of ministry banished my preconceived ideas or illusions?

- Could my hearing a call to ministry have been prompted by an unconscious longing for the parental love, acceptance, or approval I never found as a child?

- If I were successful in my search, what effect would finding the object of my search have on my life?

RUNNING FROM OR RUNNING TOWARD?

Another healthy exercise I found when working with career change was to explore whether I was running from or toward something. When I changed from being a Southern Baptist minister to a United Methodist minister, many assumed I left because of the struggle within the Southern Baptist Convention (SBC). Frankly, in the local church I was untouched by the denominational turmoil. My career change was more a movement *toward* something. I was not certain on what journey I was embarking with my family, or why, but I knew that we were not where we needed to be. In faith, my wife and I agreed to act on that intuition.

During the period in which I changed denominations, I did a great deal of psychological and spiritual work on myself and with my family. But when asked by the United Methodist Church why I was leaving my lifelong church tradition, I responded, "I am not leaving or running from something; rather I am moving toward something new." The way we frame our departure makes a difference.

It is important to remember that, at any given moment, our understanding is incomplete. We have suggested framing the career consideration in terms of moving *toward* something. But how do we know whether we are moving toward or running from something? One way is to identify recurring issues in one's life, for they are clues to the unconscious parts of ourselves or past relationships we seek to leave behind, whether they are part of our professional ministry or our personal lives. The source of this wisdom is found in the story of Esau and Jacob. At the end of Jacob's journey, he was facing unresolved issues—he had to be reconciled to the very one from whom he fled in the beginning of the journey if he was to move beyond "stuckness" to growth. When we try to run from ourselves or from some unresolved relationship that frightens us, we continue to be confronted by it.

Unresolved issues haunt us and recur in other relationships. An example from a staff conflict: I was called in to help resolve a conflict in a church in which two staff members had become fixated on one another. They were stuck together like Velcro. One's behavior determined the other's. Neither had the ability to think calmly and objectively about the situation. When they came together, emotional reactions or mindless automatic responses determined their behavior. As I worked with the two, I discovered that one had had this recurring pattern in past ministries. He would become fixated on a person in a power position and then create a conflict in an effort to get the other terminated. When the issue came to a critical point and he was forced to look more closely at his part in the conflict, he would leave the job, find somewhere else to serve, and say he was called to another place of ministry. He was running from himself and from some unresolved relationship in his past. Of course, the minister in the power position had her own unresolved issues, so her functioning aggravated his emotional reactivity. Both were living out a past unresolved relationship through this staff relationship. But the anxious one who kept moving from place to place illustrates how recurring issues or themes suggest that we are running from, not toward, something. As we explored this theme, it was traced back to unresolved issues in the staff member's family of origin. Those unresolved issues kept arising and interfering in his relationships with others. Instead of facing the issues, he kept running from them. Part of the problem concerned his search for love and acceptance at the time he had felt rejected in his early years. As we moved into his family-of-origin issues, he chose not to explore this painful chapter any further but rather to pursue another career. The past was his present. The first step in preventing the past from reconfronting us in destructive ways is to become aware of unresolved issues that reveal themselves in our patterns of behavior.

To help you consider the nature of change in your life, and if you are running from, running toward, or a little of both, reflect on the following questions.

- Am I running from something or toward something?

- What would it mean for me to face what I'm running from, as Jacob faced the stranger and Esau?

- What am I running toward?

- What professional position might match what I seek? What career description could fulfill my search? Depending on what I seek, it may be that no position will satisfy me. What I might very well need is profound healing, a change of heart, and professional help and time to move to that place of healing.

The questions suggested thus far are difficult. As you move into them, you may find new insights, some disturbing and others empowering. If some questions seem to hold more energy than you can handle right now, ask a friend or pastoral counselor to assist you in exploring these questions. I found that as I interviewed ministers, many said after the interview that they did not realize how much they needed to talk about the issue with someone else. They were stunned by the clarity that emerged after discussing it with another. As you probe your motives, do not be frightened by the questions, but listen for God to speak to you through them.

Poet and novelist D. H. Lawrence writes, "We torture ourselves getting somewhere, and when we get there it is nowhere, for there is nowhere to get to."[4] The place we are trying to reach often mirrors what we are running from, and both are often within us, where we are.

Calling and Vocation

Deep reflection into the past may yield insight into our present and future. The beginning of our story is our creation myth. Revisiting it can help us discern our place. When I was in therapy during the time I explored my life's direction, the therapist and I spent many sessions on my calling, revisiting it and the images it offered. Slowly, what I needed to hear and was ready to hear emerged. Eventually, the images became a response to the question "What have I lost and for what am I searching?" Revisiting our call may reinforce where we are, or it may inform us why we need to take another path. Either way, that calling is a wellspring out of which energy flows, insights surface, and guidance comes.

Revisit your "original call," or the time when you consciously said, "I am going into the professional ministry." Give attention to the feelings and images that arise as you relive the experience; be sensitive to the energy, watch for new insights, or go deeper into insights you have already uncovered. Ask yourself the following questions:

• What do I feel as I revisit and reflect on my original call?

- Who comes to mind as I recall my ordination or the conscious acknowledgment of my call to public, professional ministry?

- What were my original images of ministry?

- How is professional ministry different from my early expectations?

DID SOMEONE CALL?

At this early stage in your journey of discernment, "What is calling?" is another healthy question on which to reflect. Calling is a word derived from the Latin *vocare*, to call. Call, as used in mainline Christian traditions, usually refers to that first moment when a person begins to realize that a form of ministry in the institutional church will be his or her life's work. Throughout this section I use "call" and "vocation" synonymously. The way one understands calling strongly influences the way one responds to leaving or staying in the ministry of the institutional church. The more I explored it with ministers, the more I realized that for many this term has a nebulous quality.

Throughout history, different words have been used to explain the phenomenon of calling. The Romans called it genius; the Greek, *daimon* or sisters of fate; the romantic John Keats called it the heart; Neoplatonists referred to it as an imaginal body, the *ochema*, that carried one like a ve-hicle; and Christians see it as God's plan or will. Reformer John Calvin called it predestination; others image it as the current of the river into which we are invited to step but given the choice not to step, to stay safe on dry land. To accept the flow of life and step into the current of the water is to answer a call. But we are free to stay on the bank where it is safe and dry, and miss a deeper call—this choosing is free will. No matter how it has been conceptualized or imaged, the persistent need to define one's role in the world is a lifelong, soulful task, and to fulfill one's role is a calling.

Throughout history, various cultures have struggled to explain or rec-ognize calling. In primitive tribes, certain rituals, circumstances, experiences, and signs were needed to confirm the shaman's or medicine man's call; the elders confirmed the recognized gifts.

In the Christian tradition, inward call and outward recognition are nec-essary for professional clergy. Discerning one's call or granting legitimacy to another's call includes an acknowledgment of that call by other Chris-tians. According to traditional Christian theology, there are two forms of calling as it relates to professional ministry. First is the inward call, either persistent or occasional, that confronts a person as a feeling, intuition, or subjective experience. Second is the outward calling—the call a specific community extends to the individual. The outward call is confirmed by the whole church. But the personal experience and understanding of call goes beyond these simple concepts.

We encourage you to examine more deeply the nature and focus of calling. By doing so, you will be able to articulate your position and meaning more confidently for yourself and for those who desire to know about your calling. For many clergy I interviewed, ambiguity surrounded the question of calling, and they were not able to articulate an understanding of the term. Their experience and what they had been taught did not seem consistent to them. I asked clergy during the interview process, "Is calling unique to clergy and professional ministers?" Several argued that calling is not unique to clergy but is available to all people as we pursue our gifts and talents. For this group, working in the supermarket could be as much a response to a calling as stepping into the pulpit each Sunday morning. Others I inter-viewed said that some people are called to specific tasks, like Moses, Jonah, and Jesus, while others are called to live a Christian life wherever they find themselves. Yet others argued that calling as imaged by the church is more a political than a theological statement. According to this view, it is a term used by the institution to empower itself; this power regulates who discerns the clergy's calling, who may regulate the clergy, and who empowers the clergy with responsibilities in a different arena from that of the laity. Calling is understood in many ways and interpreted from various perspectives and contexts.

Sometimes we understand calling as that moment when we "hear" God saying, "You are my servant in ministry." Others frame calling as a lifelong process that brings us to a point of ministry, with no single moment that defines "the call." In seminary, a student was asked to write about his calling, and he wrote his life story, arguing that his entire life, not a particular moment, contributed to bringing him to training for the ministry. Calling is the place where God, through life, has brought us. It is the place our life's meaning, desires, and talents meet. For each individual, the experience will be different; understanding one's unique experience will assist one in interpreting possible career changes.

One source of understanding is Scripture. The Bible offers stories of callings: Jonah in the belly of the whale because he refused to go to Nineveh; Moses the stutterer, called to set God's people free, to lead them through the wilderness; Jeremiah, the doleful denouncer, lamenting to the people; Samuel, the one who heard the music three times before learning to dance; Isaiah, with singed tongue and charred lips speaking the divine words; Peter, fishing on the sea, called to follow; Paul blinded, knocked off his horse, but chosen to receive new sight; Jesus, possessed by God, thus nailed; and Judas, the zealous one, exercising the dark side of calling. In Holy Scripture and history, numerous examples and images of calling are offered; these stories attest to the uniqueness of calling even as they comfort us when we find our path to calling rocky.

Psychotherapist and writer Thomas Moore offers Jesus' baptism as an image for calling. Consider Jesus standing on the banks of the River Jordan to be baptized as he is about to begin his life's work. Moore writes:

> The scene is a portrait of a significant moment in any life: one finds oneself standing in the powerful, streaming currents of time and fate . . . among other things, it represents the stream of events and persons in which the individual finds his [or her] place. . . . It's an inspiring image of the willingness to step courageously into the river of existence, instead of finding ways to remain safe, dry, and unaffected.[5]

According to this image, calling is the river's flow, and we make the choice to step into the river of life, into its flow—and to trust where the river, or God through life's flow, takes us. That attitude is to say yes to the call. As we step into the water, we, like Jesus, hear the voice from the deep saying, "This is my beloved in whom I am well pleased." For some, Scripture, particularly passages about the life of Jesus, helps them understand their call as spiritual and specifically religious, while others understand call to be spiritual, but not always connected to a religious tradition or an institutional religious expression.

Other disciplines address this issue of calling. Speaking at a local church, author Ernest Gaines compared his writing vocation to having a block of wood on his back. Writing was his calling, his passion and burden that he had to accept. Novelist Alice Walker speaks of writing as the only thing she could do. The writer's perspective was in her from birth. Writing was her calling, an expression of a voice trying to break into the universe. Artists like Michelangelo and others express in sculpture or painting what they cannot put into words. An artist I visited said, "I paint not because I want to, but because I have to." She is called. Is this calling any different from the call to the professional ministry, or to put it differently, is any person's life work his or her calling? We ask you to consider these expansive definitions of calling as they relate to your career and understanding of vocation and career.

Let us look at several definitions or descriptions of calling from prolific cultural writers in various disciplines. These are not exhaustive, but they show us the vastness and significance of the subject. In *The Soul's Code*, archetypal psychologist James Hillman writes:

> There is more in a human life than our theories (or theologies) of it allow. Sooner or later something seems to call us onto a particular path. You may remember this something as a single moment in childhood when an urge out of nowhere, a fascination, a peculiar turn of events struck like an annunciation: This is what I must do, this is what I've got to do. This is who I am. . . . If not this vivid or sure, the call may have been more like gentle pushings in the stream in which you drifted unknowingly to a particular spot on the bank. Looking back, you sense that fate had a hand in it.[6]

According to Hillman, calling is a moment of certainty or a gentle process taking us where we need to go. Fate is the word used for that which is bigger than us, for God. Becoming conscious of this calling, however it manifests itself, is our challenge. According to Hillman, fate, or what the Judeo-Christian tradition would describe as God, is working to bring us to "a particular spot on the bank." Looking back, we see how we were brought to this place.

In *The Annie Dillard Reader*, Annie Dillard writes:

> The thing is to stalk your calling in a certain skilled and supple way, to locate the most tender and live spot and plug into that pulse. This is yielding, not fighting. A weasel doesn't "attack" anything; a weasel lives as he's meant to, yielding at every moment to the perfect freedom of single necessity.[7]

The depth psychologist Carl G. Jung writes:

> What is it, in the end, that induces a person to go their own way and to rise out of unconscious identity with the mass as out of a swathing mist? . . . It is what is commonly called vocation: an irrational factor that destines a person to emancipate themselves from the herd and from its well-worn paths. True personality is always a vocation and puts its trust in it as in God . . . vocation acts like a law of God from which there is no escape. . . . Anyone with a vocation hears the voice of the inner person: they are called.[8]

Jung suggests that a calling leads one toward one's individual way in contrast to the way of the masses. According to Jung, to hear one's inner voice from God and to be as true to it as Jesus was to his, is calling, vocation, or honoring the soul.

Then there are the words of Frederick Buechner: "The place God calls you to is the place where your deepest gladness and the world's deepest hunger meet."[9]

Calling is a metaphor, and from its metaphoric nature comes its power to move us. Various disciplines grapple with the meaning of calling. Calling is a word that conjures up images on which we can reflect as we consider our vocation, our career, and our life task. Reflect on calling, meditating on the following questions.

- How do I understand calling?

- Is considering a move to a nonreligious career as much a calling as one in the context of the institutional church?

- Theologically, do I image this calling to professional ministry as unchanging? Can calling to professional ministry change?

- For me, is moving to another career a calling toward or a move away from something?

- Could the same God who called me into professional ministry in the institutional church now be calling me into another career?

Calling, career, and vocation are about acute listening and connection, utilizing all our gifts and capacities to discern, to dance to God's music, to step into the flow of the river.

CHAPTER 2

Exploring God's Call

It is likely that you picked up this book because ministry is not exactly what you expected it to be. Perhaps you are a recent seminary graduate in your first call or appointment and you are asking yourself if this is really what you want to do with your life. Clergy are more likely to leave within the first five years of their professional ministry than at any other time.

Others of you may be reading this book because you are in midlife and you doubt that you can keep up the pace until retirement. Managing conflicts with and between people, fretting over the budget, and a host of other stressors tell you your job is too much. In addition, if your children are headed toward or already in college, you may be wondering how you can possibly pay for a college education on the one hand and prepare for your retirement on the other. You may ask, Why have I spent a career making so little money?

Whatever your chronological age and era in ministry, you may feel as if the church owns all your time and emotional energy. Some ministers believe that regardless of how much they give to a church and its people, they are always asked to give more. That's an uncomfortable feeling. When a minister feels owned, anger and depression are not far behind. Perhaps you picked this book up hoping to discover a way out of professional ministry, or at least out of a ministry you feel trapped in.

Maybe you are reading this book because you have been forced to leave professional ministry. This book may be a beginning point in attempting to find a way back to professional ministry. Perhaps you are hoping to bring closure to a particular ministry.

Some of you are judicatory personnel looking for solutions to the problems of clergy leaving professional ministry for whatever reason. I invite you to work through the book for yourself also.

Whatever reasons have brought you to this book, I am glad you are here. I have been ordained for 30 years and have struggled with all the issues cited above. I hope you will come to see me as a companion on the journey as you read and work through this book. I begin by inviting you to examine your call. Exploring your call can be an exciting adventure. Perhaps you will discover pieces of your call that you had forgotten and discern ways to continue honestly to seek God's movement in your career.

The call to ministry is both unknowable (the Mystery at work) and knowable (personal needs that make ministry appealing). Expecting some (though not all) of your personal needs to be met in ministry is realistic. You can anticipate never fully understanding all about your call because it is bigger than you (the Mystery at work). The call to ministry is discovered by individuals between our personal needs (and our attempts to meet some of these needs) and God's mystery that is never fully understood by us.

Church sociologist H. Richard Niebuhr[1] used a fourfold typology to describe the call to full-time professional, although not necessarily ordained, ministry. It is a useful tool to examine your calling. While using the basic model, I have taken today's context of ministry into account.

The call to be a Christian which comes to all believers. This call makes baptism our mandate to serve in Christ's name. It is the calling to faithful discipleship, to become a faithful witness to the love of God, particularly as this love is revealed and fleshed out in Jesus of Nazareth.

Our understanding of the call to every believer has suffered as the roles of clergy and laity have been divided and given different functions. Clergy have often taken on what can effectively be the role and task of every believer—for example, clergy who do all the caring for a congregation. Another mutation of this call to every believer has been clergy who deal with the "spiritual affairs" of the church while laity deal with the "business affairs." Of course, the false dichotomy leads to even more problems. Regardless of how this call has been abused, the call to be a Christian is where every call to professional ministry begins.

The second call in Niebuhr's fourfold typology is the secret call. In this call a person feels chosen by God to be an ordained minister. This call can be perceived only by you. In the tradition in which I was raised and ordained, many who had experienced the secret call talked about "wrestling with the call," or "running from the call." It could not be received as grace; rather, it had to be resisted and finally surrendered to. "Fighting the call" and then "surrendering to the call" were a way of saying, "This call is God's doing, not mine." It acknowledged the unknowable (the Mystery at work) while denying the knowable (personal needs that make ministry appealing).

My secret call was very different from the "running and surrendering" version. During my childhood my parents divorced. My mother went to work, and my grandmother kept house. When my grandmother became ill, I was needed to take on more adult responsibility. At the same time my church was becoming a special place to me and giving me unique opportunities for leadership. I felt special and safe in my church and with my church's leaders. That was my call to ministry. I wanted to be for someone else the support that my church family had become for me. Rather than running and surrendering, I was a rank volunteer.

Coming to terms with one's story about the secret call is essential for the minister. Often after meetings that are more about turf than kingdom-of-God work or after a day spent dealing with what seem to be trivial issues, recalling the story of your secret call can provide an anchor to keep you stabilized.

Niebuhr identifies the third call as the providential call. The providential call is discerning first one's gifts and graces and second, the type of professional ministry for which those gifts and graces make one best suited. This is the ministry for which both you and others can see you are gifted. As I grew up, the only role I knew about was parish pastor. Today the roles clergy fill are diverse and numerous, from media to business.

My best friend is a preacher/worship leader. While he functions well in the other areas of pastoral work, it is in proclamation and worship where he shines. I have spent my ministry in the specialized area of pastoral care and counseling. I have studied it, practiced it, supervised it, taught it, and written about it.

The variety of our providential calls (prison chaplain, parish pastor, seminary teacher) makes a beautiful tapestry in the ministry of the church. Paul said it this way: "A body isn't a body, unless there is more than one part—together you are the body of Christ—First, God chose some to be apostles and prophets and teachers for the church, but God also chose some..." (1 Corinthians 12:19-31 [CEV]). This phrase "But God also chose some . . ." is a way of saying that whatever your gifts and graces, they are useful to Christ's church in professional ministry.

I believe developing one's gifts and graces and honing them to a level of specialty can be useful to a minister. In a role that is diverse, having expertise in one area more than a generalization in everything can help a minister feel anchored. This specialization in one area can also be the focus of continuing education and sabbaticals. It can serve as an area in which to train other ministers, one to write about. In short, in a career that often makes people wonder if they know anything, it can assure you that you do.

The fourth call to ministry is the ecclesiastical call. This call is heard when a congregation or institution invites a minister to serve with or within the church or institution. Many ministers receive an ecclesiastical call to serve a particular congregation as pastor or in a specialized role (music, education, youth, children, pastoral counseling, or business management).

Many other ministers receive an ecclesiastical call and are endorsed by their denominational group to serve in a specialized setting other than parish ministries. My call within the United Church of Christ is as director of the pastoral counseling division of the McFarland Institute. Many others such as military and hospital chaplains, pastoral counselors, and fire and police chaplains have ecclesiastical calls to specialized settings in ministry.

If any one of these four calls is missing, a sense of unease is likely to be present in the minister:

1. The call to be a Christian.
2. The secret call.
3. The providential call.
4. The ecclesiastical call.

When you feel a sense of imbalance, returning to your personal story of call and the sources of your call will often help you gain new understanding upon which action can be taken. I invite you to examine your calling in three stages First, in the spaces below briefly write the story of your calling in each of these four areas as you would have at the time you were ordained.

1. The call to be a Christian.

2. The secret call.

3. The providential call.

4. The ecclesiastical call.

The second stage of this reflective exercise is to write the story of your calling in each of the four areas as you understand your present calling.

1. The call to be a Christian.

2. The secret call.

3. The providential call.

4. The ecclesiastical call.

Now list the changes that have occurred as a natural process of your growth through the years.

Are there discrepancies between the two that you need to examine and seek the meaning of? If so, list them here.

I invite you to discuss with a trusted friend, spiritual director, or pastoral counselor both the changes as a result of your growth and the discrepancies that are too obvious to ignore. Which person I chose would be based on the nature of the issues I wanted to discuss.

PERSONAL NEEDS AND THE CHURCH'S MINISTRY

Being conscious of the sources involved in your secret call (the call that can be perceived only by you) can be one way of examining the issue of whether you should stay in the ministry. What personal needs helped set the stage for your secret call? As described above, the need to belong laid the foundation for my secret call. There is nothing wrong with my neediness being a part of my call since God calls us as humans to serve God. But my continuing to be in denial or to stay unaware of my neediness would have great potential to harm me, others, or both. For example, if I am unaware of my unresolved grief issues, I can easily contaminate someone else's grief process rather than help them.

Which of these personal needs helped lay the foundation for your secret call?

_____ The need to belong
_____ The need for recognition
_____ The need to be controlled
_____ The need not to be controlled
_____ The need for power

_____ The need to have a respected community role
_____ The need to have meaning in life
_____ The need to avoid failure
_____ Other (specify) _____
_____ Other (specify) _____
_____ Other (specify) _____

If you were to accept and begin working toward fulfilling your unmet personal needs, with what needs would you start?

Which needs in your checklist have been partially if not totally met?

These unmet needs have likely in part formed the foundation of your secret calling to ministry. The more you become aware of these needs and work toward understanding and fulfilling these needs, the healthier foundation your ministry (and life) can have.

EXPLORING MY PROVIDENTIAL CALL

Personal needs are not the only factor that influences your calling. Understanding the needs of the church can also influence it. Matching your gifts and graces with the church's need is what Niebuhr called the providential call. This is the call to a ministry for which both you and others can see you are gifted. I invite you to reexamine your providential call using the reflective exercise below. Pastoral ministry (regardless of whether you are a solo pastor, senior pastor, church musician, religious educator, age-group minister, or specialized minister) consists of three major duties: proclaiming, leading, and caring. At some point you matched your gifts and graces with a need or needs of the church and answered what Niebuhr called the providential call.

How you have experienced these three pastoral tasks and which ones you responded to are important in reevaluating your call today. Mark the needs of the church you responded to in particular.

Proclamation needs of the church include:
_____ Preparation and delivery of sermons
_____ Sacramental ministry
_____ Church music, both vocal and instrumental
_____ Evangelism
_____ Calling people to justice
_____ Christian education
_____ The ministry of writing
_____ Other (specify) _____

Leadership needs of the church include:
_____ Casting and communicating a vision
_____ Leading effective meetings
_____ Managing church business affairs
_____ Developing effective procedures
_____ Training officers, boards, and committees
_____ Other (specify) _____

Care needs of the church include:
_____ Caring for the ill
_____ Caring for new members
_____ Caring for the grieving
_____ Caring for the homebound
_____ Pastoral counseling
_____ Spiritual guidance
_____ Other (specify) _____

Obviously some of these church needs cross lines (for example, sacramental ministry is both proclamation and care). Also these lists are by no means exhaustive.

Now go through the same list again and mark the needs of the church you feel you are responding to and meeting today with the greatest joy.

Proclamation:
_____ Preparation and delivery of sermons
_____ Sacramental ministry
_____ Church music, both vocal and instrumental
_____ Evangelism
_____ Calling people to justice
_____ Christian education
_____ The ministry of writing
_____ Other (specify) _____

Leadership:
_____ Casting and communicating a vision
_____ Leading effective committee meetings
_____ Managing church business affairs
_____ Developing effective procedures
_____ Training officers, boards and committees
_____ Other (specify) _____

Care:
_____ Caring for the ill
_____ Caring for new members
_____ Caring for the grieving
_____ Caring for the homebound
_____ Pastoral counseling
_____ Spiritual guidance
_____ Other (specify) _____

Keeping your awareness of your providential call (the matching of your gifts and graces to the needs of the church) current and up to date is essential for satisfaction in ministry. Since you are a living, growing human being, your gifts and graces will match different church needs in different eras of your ministry.

Roles are also crucial to satisfaction in ministry. Roles are another way to examine the providential call. Some people know from early days exactly what role they want to pursue in ministry. Others of us experiment with a variety of roles before settling in to a preferred role. Roles in ministry have also multiplied since the days when calling and pastor were synonymous. Listed below are some roles in ministry. Which of these have you tried on and which ones interest you?

Have tried	*Want to try*	
_____	_____	Pastor
_____	_____	Minister of music
_____	_____	Christian educator
_____	_____	Age group minister, preschool
_____	_____	Age group minister, children
		Age group minister, teens
_____	_____	Missionary
_____	_____	Journalist
_____	_____	Military chaplain
_____	_____	Pastoral counselor in the local church
		(specialized credentials)
_____	_____	Hospital chaplain
_____	_____	Pastoral counselor, private practice
_____	_____	Editor
_____	_____	College or seminary professor
_____	_____	Church recreation
_____	_____	Pastoral care, local church
		(staff minister to visit ill, bereaved, etc.)
		Church business administrator
_____	_____	Other (specify) _____
_____	_____	Other (specify) _____
_____	_____	Other (specify) _____

Often the minister who is unfulfilled in ministry need look no further than his or her current role to find the source of the discontent. Retraining may be necessary to find a preferred role.

One area to check when you are feeling dissatisfaction in ministry: How up to date is your understanding of your providential call? If you are feeling restless or anxious about your ministry, you might want to reexamine your providential call and see if your satisfaction level rises. If you have left ministry and are considering reentry, a reexamination of your providential call will likely be very helpful.

Exploring My Preferred Setting and Role

Niebuhr did not talk about finding one's preferred setting, yet I have come to believe that this task is important to finding satisfaction and fulfillment in ministry. In real estate the mantra is "Location! Location! Location!" In ministry, location may not be everything, but it is important. Although television and shopping malls may have served to make sections of the country less distinct, important cultural differences persist in various regions of the country.

Culture is important. Recently a pastor who was raised and educated in the West moved to the deep South. Within a few months the honeymoon was over. He was complaining about how shortsighted people in the South were. I heard him say, "Back home the sky is the ceiling!" His church members were frustrated that he was acting like the Lone Ranger, riding off and doing whatever he wanted to with no consultation from trusted church bodies and trusted church leaders. Within several years he had decided that this move was a mistake and that he needed "to get back across the Mississippi where I understand folks." His southern church members provided beans and coffee for his journey home!

This example is in no way meant to imply that ministers can't move successfully from region to region and serve the church. It is to say that it needs to be done with eyes and hearts wide open!

The year was 1974, and I was a candidate at a church in Indiana. My wife (then my fiancée) and I spent a weekend with the pastoral search committee, with an intensive interview time scheduled for Saturday evening. We gathered at a committee member's home, shared a wonderful meal and then waited two hours to begin the interview until the high-school semi-state basketball tournament being broadcast on television was over! I was an irate Southerner. My fiancée (who grew up in the Midwest) explained to me that in Indiana, interviewing a pastoral candidate paled beside the state basketball championship. I was called to the church in part because I had a cultural interpreter. I had several good years of ministry before moving on.

Before choosing to leave the ministry, examine your regional, geographic, and cultural preferences and see if your present location matches the kind of setting where you feel most comfortable.

Location (as in rural or urban, town or city) is also important. One of my best friends and I met while we both served the national church as editors and consultants. He always told me his best pastoral experiences for both himself and his family were in small towns. He now serves a small-town church and reports being more fulfilled in ministry than he ever re-members. A part of that fulfillment comes from being in a preferred setting. On the other hand, the candidate for the church I currently serve as interim is interested in part because the church is in an urban area. She is in touch with the fact that location is important.

Denomination can also be a source of discontent. Although it often goes unspoken, the minister's denomination can be a significant source of dissatisfaction. In the past decade some denominations have worked to undermine or eliminate the role of female clergy. For the woman who knows she is called by God and gifted for ministry, this restricted environment is likely to be very frustrating.

Feelings of being denominationally homeless are likely to arise for the minister who feels a passion for justice within a denomination that does not emphasize God's standing with the poor or equal treatment regardless of race, gender, or sexual orientation.

Judicatory heads and bodies that care for students through the ordination process need to communicate carefully the culture of their denomination. Knowing the culture of other denominational groups and being willing to introduce a good candidate who may be in a denomination he or she would not prefer would be a strong act of caring.

CHECKING UP ON MY CALL: DISSATISFIED OR UNFULFILLED?

Here is a checklist of things to consider before you make any moves. You may want to discuss these issues with a pastoral counselor or trusted spiritual director in your community to see if that person hears or sees things you do not.

_____ How do I describe my call to be a Christian?

_____ What do I recall about my secret call to ministry?

_____ How have I matched my gifts and graces with the church's need (the providential call)?

_____ Have I reexamined my providential call as I have grown and changed?

_____ If not, do I want to reexamine it?

_____ Which of my ecclesiastical calls has been most satisfying? Why?

_____   What personal needs laid the foundation for my secret call?
_____   Which of these personal needs, if any, are still unmet?
_____   How fully do I understand the culture of the people I minister to?
_____   Am I (and my family) living in our preferred section of the
_____   country (Northeast, Southeast, Southwest, West, Midwest)? If
       not, do I have a cultural interpreter?
       ___ Yes ___ No
_____   Am I (and my family) living in our preferred location (rural,
       urban, small town, open country)?
_____   Am I in my preferred ministry role?
_____   Am I a member of my preferred denomination?

A thorough examination of these issues before deciding whether to leave or stay in ministry will help you make a clear decision.

EXPLORING MY SPIRITUALITY

Many of us who are ministers have discovered to our amazement that we have lost a sense of the holy stirring in our lives. We might benefit greatly from exploring our spirituality as a part of grappling with hard vocational choices.

My quest for a deeper spirituality has often begun in a desert time of my life. Go to the desert with me. Psalm 103 praises the God who forgives, heals, protects and redeems. It is one of my favorite psalms because it tells the story of God's loving-kindness. One phrase that tells the story is "You redeem me from the pit" (verse 4, CEV). Even though the pit is a synonym for Sheol, surely the author and early reader were reminded of God's redeeming Joseph from the pit, his journey from Israel to Egypt, and his job of making the dream become a reality as he served as the storage administrator in Egypt during the seven years of plenty. (See Genesis 37-50 for the full story.)

Joseph's kinspeople prospered in Egypt until there came a Pharaoh who "knew not Joseph." Then the people of Israel were enslaved, becoming brickmakers. God called a reluctant freedom fighter in Moses, who after a burning bush that couldn't be put out, after plagues, the miracle of the Passover, the parting of the Red Sea, and the failed pursuit by Pharaoh's army's, led Israel to freedom—and the desert. (See Exodus 1-15 for the full story.) Exodus 15:22 states, "After the Israelites left the Red Sea, Moses led them through the Shur Desert for three days before finding water" (CEV). Three days turned into 40 years. I identify with this story, for I too have experienced being simultaneously free and in the desert.

Deciding who you are and what you are called to do is the strength of desert spirituality. The slaves of Egypt were known for what they did (excellent brickmaking). Our state of slavery is often the same; we are known for what we do well. "She's a great preacher" or "He's a wonderful pastoral counselor" are statements about what we do.

Desert spirituality teaches us to know who we are. We are Beloved of God. The desert strips us of all our pretenses. In the desert we are hot, thirsty, and hungry. In the desert we have a longing that our positions, degrees, bank accounts, and family can't satisfy. God alone is enough. The desert is an invitation to be alone with God.

Before going to the desert the Israelites were slaves in Egypt. Their lives were driven by someone else's needs and values. As slaves, the Israelites lost the Sabbath because they worked every day (only the free could awaken and ponder what they would do today). Slaves are forced to live by their master's time rather than by God's time. I know several ministers who spend their time supporting the values of others (the treasurer, the congregational president, or the denomination) rather than finding and acting upon their own values based on their understanding of kingdom values. The desert is a place of invitation to discover who you are in relationship to God (Beloved) and who you are in relationship to yourself (a free person in God's sight or a slave to others). In this discovery time you begin spending time on your own values, as discerned in time spent with God, rather than the values of others. It is the difference between slavery and freedom. This journey with God to uncharted territory offers the opportunity for transformation.

Reviewing one's life calling is most often a journey into a desert because a task so important requires enough distance to be reflective. It is a journey that takes courage because you may have to change. The journey is necessary if transformation is to take place. I admire the courage of those of you reading this book who are looking honestly at yourselves amid the process of reviewing your place in ministry. The desert is often an uncomfortable place to be; it can also be a beautiful and serene place.

Most of us make the journey more than once. You don't have to make this desert journey alone—let me offer two things: my story and several guideposts for finding a spiritual director to help you through this desert time and beyond.

Companions on the Journey: My (and Your) Story

Growing up in the deep South allowed me three religious choices; don't go to church, be a Baptist, or be a Methodist. Perhaps I could have been a snake handler, but my faith has never been that great.

Being born into a Baptist household, I became a birthright Baptist. Yes, I did have to walk down the aisle and make my own profession of faith in Jesus as Savior and Lord, and I did have to be baptized by total immersion. However, having been born into a Baptist family, I never had a choice—I am a birthright Baptist.

In high school I felt "called to preach" (the only form of ministry I knew), and by 18, while a college freshman, I became pastor of a church. College graduation led to seminary (a Baptist one, of course). During seminary I began seeking a richer religious experience. This search led me to one of my Baptist seminary professors, who led me to Quaker theologian Elton Trueblood, who led me to Earlham School of Religion. Thus began my experience of spending two years living among Friends. Even after 25 years I continue to interpret the importance of those years for me.

Already I can see I have not been alone. After writing this much of my story I can recall members of the church I was raised in, college professors who took an interest in me, seminary professors who served as mentors, and others who were companions to me in my early spiritual journey. Below recall those who helped you on your journey.

Childhood Years

The gifts these people gave me were:

TEENAGE YEARS

The gifts these people gave me were:

COLLEGE YEARS

The gifts these people gave me were:

SEMINARY YEARS

The gifts these people gave me were:

After graduating from Earlham, I earned a doctoral degree in psychology and counseling. Then I went to work for my denomination. During 12 years of employment I was editor of the national church's preaching journal and the pastoral care and counseling consultant.

During those 12 years I saw my denomination fall to the fundamentalists. It seemed to me we were becoming the culture's caricature of us as narrow-minded, bigoted, and more. I was in a crisis that led to a wilderness experience.

I began watching friends whom I admired being fired from their denominational jobs because they were on the wrong political side. My grief became overwhelming.

Using the numbers below, list friends and acquaintances you have seen experience difficult times in ministry, including yourself, and answer the subsequent questions. (Use additional sheets of paper if needed.) For the fourth item, write your own name in the space, and reflect on how you have helped yourself and what gifts you have given yourself.

MINISTERIAL COMPANIONS IN CRISIS

1. _____

What I did to help this person.

What unexpected gift (intangible) did I receive from him or her?

2. _____

What I did to help this person:

What unexpected gift (intangible) did I receive from this person?

3. _____

What I did to help this person:

What unexpected gift (intangible) did I receive from this person?

4. _____

What I have done to help myself:

What unexpected gift (intangible) have I given myself?

I knew I could no longer work for the denomination and maintain my integrity. I did believe I could serve a local church, and was called to a large Baptist congregation. I served there for five years, realizing as every year passed that an ultraconservative judgmental spirit had invaded all ranks and levels of my denomination's life, from the national boards and agencies to the local churches and associations. I had entered the desert.

I began searching for my future—spiritually and professionally. My professional life was easier to sort through. In the late 1980s I began the training process to become a pastoral counselor certified by the American Association of Pastoral Counselors and licensed by the state. Already holding an accredited doctoral degree in psychology and counseling made a new career possible. Professionally I was in a different land; it wasn't the desert, but neither did it feel like an oasis.

Denominationally the search has been much harder. During the search it became apparent to me that involvement in and identification with a denomination is important to me. It also became apparent that the tangible celebration of the sacraments of baptism and Holy Communion were important to me. I wanted a denomination that could honor my long, deep Baptist history and be flexible enough to receive me fully into the family. I found this welcome in the United Church of Christ (UCC) after years of desert wandering. I have found new companions.

MINISTERIAL COMPANIONS THROUGH THE YEARS

The gifts these people gave me were:

PRESENT-DAY COMPANIONS

The gifts I am receiving from them are:

Simultaneously with my search for a new ministry and a new denomination, I began searching for a spirituality that is a product of my adult faith. My search led me to two traditions with much in common. One of these traditions is a monastic order of the Roman Catholics; the other is Quaker (the Religious Society of Friends). These two traditions hold at least two spiritual disciplines in common. One is radical listening; the other is radical hospitality.

The part of Roman Catholic tradition that has helped nurture and form me is the Benedictine way of life. Benedict lived in the sixth century during a time of social upheaval. He began a monastery and wrote a Rule (a common discipline) that over time became the guide for most monastic communities.

The Benedictine Rule begins with the word "Listen!" Seven times a day Benedict's monks would listen to and for the Holy as they prayed the Psalms together. On the day you read this, contemplative monastics will gather to pray the Psalms and sit in silence as they listen for God's voice. Just so on First Day (Sunday) Quakers gather with others to listen for God's voice. Listening in the quiet for God is a radical ideal in a noisy culture. Daily I pray the morning office (called Liturgy of the Hours) and sit in silence listening for God's voice. The practice reminds me both that all time is holy and that as God's child it is important that I listen for God's voice.

The Benedictine and Quaker communities share at least one more commonality that guides my adult faith. In the Rule, Benedict instructed the guestmaster and the community to "receive all as if they are Christ" (chapter 53:1). Society of Friends founder George Fox urged his followers to recognize "that of God in every person." Radical hospitality marks both Benedictine and Quaker spirituality.

Radical listening and hospitality are marks of my mature faith. Being a part of traditions that honor radical listening and hospitality is important to me. Once again I have discovered companions on my spiritual journey. This time they are historical figures who continue to shape the life of the church. In the same way that St. Benedict and George Fox have been my companions, who have been your historical companions? The message is, even as you struggle with complex vocational issues, you do not have to be alone. List your historical companions on the following page.

HISTORICAL COMPANIONS

1. Companions from Scripture

The gift I have received from these companions is:

2. Companions from church history:

The gift I have received from these companions is:

3. Companions from other sources (holy writings, literature, etc.):

The gift I have received from these companions is:

Before we move on to a final kind of companion (the spiritual guide), I invite you to take a relationship inventory. If you find yourself feeling a need for more companions on the journey, what steps can you take to form the relationships you need? Some steps could be to reactivate old relationships that once were meaningful, to be mindful of people around you who act as if they want to be your friend, to keep regular contact with your mentors, or to locate a mentor. Historical companions and their value are often overlooked. If you were to choose a companion from history, who might it be?

FINDING A SPIRITUAL GUIDE

Spiritual directors are holy listeners[2] who are trained to listen with the directee to what God is saying. The ministry of spiritual direction, while rooted in the Roman Catholic tradition, currently moves across denominational lines and is an international movement. As the July 20, 1998, *Wall Street Journal* reported, "Spiritual Directors Get Popular." Spiritual Directors International, an ecumenical network of spiritual directors, has doubled in size since 1995, listing 3,200 directors in its most recent membership directory. Seeking a spiritual guide is an age-honored practice in the Christian church. As you are on your journey, you may want to solicit the aid of another as together you listen for the sound of God's stirrings in your life.

Kathleen Flood, O.P., reminds us that spiritual direction is a journey from the absurd (from the Latin word *surdus*, meaning deaf) to obedient listening. Spiritual deafness is prevalent in our day because of the noise around us, our own overactivity, and the rush of our responsibilities. When life is totally full and you are feeling unfulfilled, a spiritual director can help you move away from deafness (the absurd) toward obedience.

If you are in a time of examining your calling and vocation, seeking a spiritual director to help you listen and remember that God has called you Beloved may be important.

QUALITIES OF A SPIRITUAL DIRECTOR

If you are seeking a spiritual director, these qualities seem significant to seek out:

1. *Someone who is grounded in his or her own faith tradition.* Sitting with a person who is grounded in faith without rigid dogmatism is grounding to the directee also. Spiritual direction assumes a faith dimension in both director and directee.

2. *Someone who has excellent empathic listening skills.* Spiritual direction is not psychotherapy, yet many of the skills are common to both therapists and spiritual directors. You will want someone who respects your uniqueness and your story.

3. *Someone who is nonjudgmental.* Spiritual direction is not about changing you. It is about listening to you and with you for God's stirrings.

4. *Someone who can set aside his or her own needs.* The ministry of spiritual direction assumes enough emotional and spiritual health that a safe, secure space can be given to you, the directee.

5. *Someone who can set and maintain clear boundaries.* As in pastoral counseling, boundary issues are important in spiritual direction. Directors needs to know their own level of expertise and when they are bumping that line, how to honor time, and how to maintain confidentiality.

Finding a director you feel comfortable sitting with and talking to is essential to a helpful experience. Asking pastors or friends about their spiritual directors is one way to proceed. Another information source is schools or programs for spiritual directors. Another is your diocese or other regional judicatory. Yet another source is Spiritual Directors International, 1329 Seventh Ave., San Francisco CA 94122-2507. The organization lists directors by geographic regions.

Reaching out for help during a transition time is a sign of health. I suggest that you use career counselors and others to aid your decision-making during this time. Also be aware that in ministerial calling there are spiritual issues to be attentive to, such as, "Is God calling me to ministry?" Spiritual directors are gifted and called to help you examine yourself and your calling and to discover the stirrings of God's spirit in both.

EXPLORING YOUR FEELINGS

If Forrest Gump's mother had told him, "Life is like a den of rattlesnakes," Forrest would have most likely had a very different life than he had since his Mother told him, "Life is like a box of chocolates."[3] The stories we hear (and believe) are most often given great power to shape our lives. What stories have you heard and believed about ministry? Fill in the incomplete sentences below:

Church members will always

Be careful working with a vestry (session, church council, diaconate) because

Complete this sentence as if you are the new pastor of this church.

The last three pastors of this church were

but I am

As you completed these sentences, what feelings came to the surface? Did you feel glad? Sad? Mad? Guilty? Scared? I hope you were able to discern that how you completed the story was connected to the ensuing feeling. Exploring how your feelings are linked to stories that have more than one possible ending and seeing your power to create more effective stories for yourself may empower you as you determine your place in ministry. Let's try one story with three different endings.

1. If I leave the ministry,

(Complete this with an ending you perceive to be negative.)

2. If I leave the ministry,

(Complete this with an ending you perceive to be neutral.)

3. If I leave the ministry,

(Complete this with an ending you perceive to be positive.)

The stories you (or the culture) write about yourself—and the meanings you assign to those stories—have great power in your life.

Many ministers understand the power of stories. In the Judeo-Christian faith, God is the God of the story. The creation story, God's saving story of God's people and others, tells us who we are as a faith community.

In the same way, we need to deconstruct the stories and then clear out a space to reflect on the stories' meaning for us. To deconstruct a story, begin asking reflective questions such as, "Whose story is this?" "Why is this story important to them to keep?" "What would happen if the story was given up?" Ask these questions now of the statement: "Women can't be pastors." Now that you have reflected on this statement, how can we write a new story about the topic of women in ministry? The process of "restorying":

- Locates the problem outside of you, the minister.
- Observes the culture the story is a part of.
- Takes the story apart to see how it affects you and others.
- Allows you to rewrite the story in a way that is helpful to you and those around you.

Now let's use a second illustration. Bob grew up hearing that Christians in general and ministers in particular should never get angry. As an adult in ministry he finds he can't live up to the story that "ministers never get angry"; thus he often feels guilty.

If Bob lives with that story and never deconstructs it, his ministry can be filled with misery by this unexamined story. In deconstructing the story, some questions to ask might be:

- How does this story (ministers should never feel angry) help and hurt our culture?
- When does the fact that I can't live up to the story seem most apparent to me?
- What do I do as a result of my struggle with this story that I wouldn't do otherwise?
- How does this problem affect:

  1. My attitudes and behaviors toward myself?
  2. My attitudes and behaviors toward others?
  3. My work, social and family life?

Locating problems outside of yourself ("Feeling guilty causes me trouble") rather than inside yourself ("I am a problem") and deconstructing the problem in a more manageable way (perhaps "never getting angry is an unrealistic expectation" rather than "I feel guilty because I as a minister should never get angry" in this case) helps Bob write a new story that is his own rather than latch onto an unexamined story in the culture. Some deconstructing questions to ask are:

- Do I think unrealistic expectations have affected other clergy?
- When unrealistic expectations made an appearance in my life, how did they affect me?
- Did I struggle with unrealistic expectations before I became a Christian educator?

Another example of the process is to write a new story around the dilemma. Rather than focus on when the problem has overcome you, you can focus on when you have overcome the problem. Some revisionist questions to ask yourself if you are doing this might be:

- What strategies have I used to fight this feeling of unrealistic expectations?
- When I reframe this story, how will my feelings about myself change?
- As I win more battles against these feelings of unrealistic expectations, how will my life look in the future?
- Five years from now, how will I be thinking about myself as a person?
- If I were to tell others about my successes, how would I describe myself?
- Now that I have made this new commitment (not to let unrealistic expectations harm me and my life), what will my spouse most notice that is new?
- What do I know about my victory that I would like to share with other clergy?

Becoming the author of your emotional life is helpful and healthy regardless of the career choice you make. Narrative therapy gives you access to your story and what you want to revise.

KNOWING AND NOT KNOWING THE WAY

Ministry and the search for vocational clarity are a great deal like Abraham and Sarah leaving Ur for a new home. Wandering can be both exhilarating and frightening. Wanderers may both know where they are going (a city not made with hands) and yet not know.

CHAPTER 3

Managing Anxiety in Times of Change

Aminister named Mary called to tell me that she was preparing to change careers. We talked about her desire to make a change and the path she intended to follow. Then Mary asked, "How does my family fit into all this?" Because she is part of a family system, I said, her family was already involved in the transition. People do not have the choice of whether to involve family. The question one must ask is, How do we as clergy involve our families, friends, and colleagues in a positive way in the process of change or transition?

A family systems perspective asserts that all of us live in emotional systems and that we are deeply connected with those around us. Consequently, to understand the individual, we look at him or her in relationship to the entire emotional system and the person's position in it. We look at the whole, not only the parts. Psychiatrist and family systems theorist Murray Bowen once likened a systems perspective to the view of a football game from the roof of a stadium rather than from a seat on the 50-yard line. Educator and writer Margaret Wheatley offers a wonderful illustration of systems theory.

> I recently heard from my son's fifth grade teacher that the largest living organism on the planet lives in Utah, where we now live. My son got excited and thought it was Bigfoot, but it's not. It is a grove of aspen trees that covers thousands of acres. When we look at them we think, "Oh, look at all the trees." When botanists looked underground they said, "Oh, look at this system, it's all one. This is one organism." You see, when aspen trees propagate, they don't send out seeds or cones, they send out runners, and a runner runs for the light (there's wonderful imagery in all of this), and we say

"Aha! There's another tree . . ." until we look underground, and we see that it is all one vast connection.[1]

We find an example of the interconnectedness of a family system in Scott, a minister undergoing a change in careers. When he came by my office to talk about his transition, he told me that his family was handling his transition well. The family was having some struggles, but very minimal ones. In fact, the family, according to Scott's interpretation, was doing so well that I wondered if his perception was accurate. As we were talking, he said, "I have to go run my son to the doctor. He's older than the 'normal' age for it, but he still wets the bed. The doctor once said his bladder was probably too small, and if the bed-wetting continued, I should bring him back so we could take some steps to stop it." A light went on in my head. We began to discuss anxiety in the family and how it sometimes surfaces in strange ways. I asked, "Could the bed-wetting be the result of the anxiety in the family surfacing through your son?" He responded, "I don't think so, but I guess it is possible."

One month after Scott had settled into his new situation, his son stopped wetting the bed. This outcome hardly seems a coincidence.

Even though we appear separate, a strong connection resides between us. Our family is an intricately connected emotional system; therefore, what affects one person in the system has an effect on the rest of the system. Mary's question about her family's involvement in this time of change was on the mark.

ANXIETY IN THE SYSTEM

To move through a time of change in a healthy way, we must manage the anxiety in the emotional system. Anxiety is a basic human emotion and part of every relational system. It is, according to Michael Kerr, director of the Georgetown University Family Center, "the response of the organism to a threat, real or imagined."[2] The word anxiety comes from a Latin root that means to cause pain by squeezing, to have by the throat, "to choke, to cause distress," to strangle.[3] Anxiety can be acute or chronic. Acute anxiety is a response to a real, immediate threat. Chronic anxiety is more imaginal and surfaces around "what if" questions not grounded in reality. When anxiety is high, families and individuals are less calm, responsive, reflective, and objective, and more reactive and emotional. Anxiety and emotional reactivity are processes not easily distinguishable, so we use these terms interchangeably.

Recently I had a computer expert install antivirus software on my computer. After he had completed the job, I asked, "Where is it?" He responded, "It is in the background running. You won't see it until the right conditions constellate through a virus entering the system. Then it'll surface and become visible." Anxiety in our emotional systems is like that antivirus program—always there and in the background running, but surfacing or becoming visible only when certain conditions trigger it. Anxiety is triggered in many ways; transitions such as career moves may activate it.

Managing or regulating the anxiety within the family or other network of friends or colleagues is a critical part of a minister's healthy transition. When anxiety rises or conditions bring chronic anxiety to the surface, certain behaviors are activated.

First, in anxious families the members are highly reactive to one another, lacking the ability to remain calm and objective in the face of collective anxiety. Mary spoke of her family's tendency toward highly intense conflict at times of transition. For example, when one of her daughters made a comment, the other reacted strongly, and then the entire family got involved, shouting and overreacting to a simple misunderstanding. Each was reacting to the other, and no one in the family maintained a sense of calm and objectivity. This reactivity is a characteristic of high anxiety.

Second, anxious families develop relational triangles. They extend the anxiety between two people and draw in a third person or issue. Triangles allow us to place or displace the anxiety. Displacing anxiety on another person is an unhealthy response that has adverse effects. Gossip, affairs, sibling conflicts, and occasions when the youngest and oldest "gang up" against the middle are examples of triangles.

When Susan, a minister, was thinking of leaving her full-time position as associate pastor of a large, demanding parish and taking a part-time position as a nursing-home chaplain, she and her husband, John, also a minister, had painful and sometimes heated discussions about what the drop in her income would mean for the household budget. As a result, they became child-focused, placing their anxiety and energy as a couple on their teenage son, Jason, to keep from dealing with their own relationship. The couple stabilized, but when they placed the anxiety on Jason, he became the person through whom the anxiety surfaced. He became for the parents what psychologists call the "identified patient"—that is, the family member designated as having the problem. When Jason became the focus of the system, he began to drink heavily. The systemic anxiety was surfacing *through* Jason, not *because* of Jason. At first, the family focused on Jason's drinking as his problem until Susan and John were forced to look at the situation as a whole, and ask, "What is really going on? Is this an individual issue, or a systemic one?" The parents were healthy enough to acknowledge their level of functioning and the position in which they had placed Jason. Painfully, they began to take responsibility for their functioning, for the way they had positioned Jason in the emotional system, and how they had *triangulated* him. Then they began the path to healing. Triangulation can be a sign of an anxious system; it can have crippling effects on family members if allowed to continue unchecked.

Third, when families become anxiety-driven, forces of togetherness activate. Bowen observed that when anxiety pervades a family, friends, or colleagues, the pull toward togetherness is dominant. Everyone is pressured to think and act as one. Diversity and individuality are not encouraged.

Fourth, secrets, covert operations, and hidden agendas are other signs of rising anxiety in the family. Secrets between anxious family members impede healthy change.

The destructive effect of secrets can be seen in the story of Lewis, a minister going through a transition. Lewis and his wife, Jill, had financial difficulties because of unexpected expenses, so Lewis, without Jill's knowledge or consent, took out a second mortgage on their home. Not knowing their financial situation, Jill continued her accustomed spending habits. She discovered the second mortgage by accident, through a letter left open on a desk. Trust had been violated, and serious work was required to move through this secret and the wounds it caused. Open communication promotes healthy transition.

Fifth, in an anxious system, family members lose a sense of humor and playfulness, demand certainty, and blame others both in the family and outside it for their own choices. When these behaviors surface, anxiety is high, and trouble is near.

When my family and I were going through our transition, we reminded ourselves regularly that we were facing the struggles and anxiety because of our choices, not because we were victims of other people. Blame and displacement escalate anxiety and create greater chaos in the family and other relationships. As we took responsibility for our choices and our own happiness, the family stabilized and the anxiety lessened.

Sixth, when the family becomes anxious, sabotage is a natural response to change. Systemically, when the minister is challenging the relationship system through a career change, the natural response of family members is resistance. Families and other systems naturally react to change by trying to maintain their form or balance (homeostasis). Resistance to change is sabotage. Rabbi Edwin Friedman, a family psychologist, said that the key to the kingdom is learning to deal with sabotage. Career change upsets the balance in the family and other relationships, and resistance is an automatic response. The key is not the resistance but one's ability to respond to it nonanxiously and creatively.

For example, when my wife began graduate school, another form of transition for the family, our son said to her, "I don't like your going to school. You never spend time with me." My wife calmly evaluated what he said, discussed it with him, made certain she did spend time with him, and continued moving toward her goal by working on her degree. Whenever change occurs, the balance in the system is upset, and resistance is the outcome. How we respond to sabotage determines whether the change is going to be a building block for growth and maturity or a path to regression and reactivity.

When anxiety remains at a high level over time, the issues or content become secondary and the anxiety primary. To return to the issues one must first work to lower or regulate family anxiety. Working on one's own functioning in the emotional system is a primary way to regulate the swirling anxiety and to restore health to the family.

Mary learned that when her family became emotionally reactive, if she could stay nonanxious, calm, and objective, the system's anxiety regulated itself and the reactivity was minimized. As a result, the family moved forward through the conflict rather than becoming stuck.

EMOTIONAL FIELDS

Another way to think about anxiety in the family system is to use a concept developed by psychiatrist Murray Bowen: All relationship systems are emotional fields. A field is an environmental force, like a gravitational field. The difference between gravitational fields and emotional fields is that people have the capacity to see and influence an emotional field by their functioning in it—that is, whenever two people come together, an emotional field results. Are we conscious enough to determine the field, or does it determine us? When anxiety escalates, whether among family members, friends, or colleagues, the emotional field gains power and determines the behavior of those in it.

Think about what happens, for example, when we go home to our family of origin. The behavioral and emotional shifts that take place when we enter that space are often quite severe. I remember noticing that my parents suddenly changed when they returned to their families of origin. They assumed the family roles they had played growing up. My wife and I act similarly when we visit our parents, brothers, and sisters. It takes a mature, self-aware person not to get caught in the emotional field or anxiety, and even more strength and maturity to influence the emotional field we enter.

When we undergo transition as clergy, we and our families and any other emotional systems to which we are connected experience anxiety, and the unstable emotional field can lead to or draw out of us unhealthy, mindless, automatic, reactive behaviors. The challenge is to recognize when the emotional field is determining our behavior and we are becoming reactive. We then need to try to get enough emotional distance and objectivity to bring calm to the family so that it and we can relate in healthy ways.

OUR PETS AS PART OF THE FAMILY

Let us not forget that pets are part of our family as well. In one case study, a minister was terminated from a church position. He took the dismissal as a blow to his self-worth and self-esteem and lost the confidence to make family decisions. His wife had never acted as the family decision-maker or leader. Their dog, Lady, began to misbehave. At 10:00 every evening, she would go around the room and nip each of them to get them to bed. If the family had company, Lady would do the same to all present. She also became possessive of the kitchen. The couple took Lady to a veterinarian and discovered that her response reflected the fact that no person in the family was taking the leadership position. As a result, the pet assumed that role. Until one of the adults took on the position of head of the family, the pet would continue her dogged leadership. When the adults were coached to reestablish themselves in the leadership position by making decisions, the problem with the dog's nipping at people and possessing the kitchen stopped.

The systems in which we live have an effect not only on the people, but possibly on all parts of the emotional system, including our pets.

MOVING THE FAMILY THROUGH TIMES OF CHANGE

We turn now to the question, "How can I, as a minister, undergo transition in a way that minimizes the negative effect on my family system, namely my spouse, children, family of origin, friends, colleagues, and even pets? How can we grow from the change, rather than be torn apart by it?"

DIFFERENTIATION

First, when we undergo change in our careers, the key task is to maintain self within the system while staying connected with the other members. Differentiation involves defining the self while staying connected to others. In Bowen's family systems theory, differentiation and leadership are synonymous. Being differentiated involves at least five components that take a lifetime of work to develop. These are:

- To be able to make "I" statements and take "I" positions in the family and other emotional systems.
- To know where I am headed, to have a direction.
- To know what I believe, what my convictions are, and to be able to articulate them in a way that is not belittling to those who believe differently.
- To know where I stop and others begin, to maintain boundaries.
- To have the emotional maturity to distinguish within myself the difference between what Murray Bowen calls intellectual functioning and emotional functioning.

Bowen distinguishes between responses that raise emotional reactivity and escalate anxiety and those that lower the anxiety through a higher level of functioning, one that is calm, reflective, objective, nonanxious, and nonreactive.

The best illustration I have found of differentiation is a fable by Friedman titled "The Bridge."[4] A man is on a journey. A stranger with a rope around his waist meets him on a bridge. The stranger gives the man on the journey the end of the rope and says, "Whatever happens, do not let go of the rope." Then the stranger jumps off the bridge. He is dangling below, and the journeyer standing on the bridge cries out, "Why did you jump off the bridge?" The man below says, "Never mind that; my life is in your hands, so do not let go." The journeyer on the bridge cannot pull the other up because their weight is perfectly counterbalanced. Finally, after much talk, the journeyer devises a way for the stranger below to save himself. The journeyer explains the plan to the stranger below. The dangling man can slowly pull himself up, wrap the rope around his waist, then rest. He can do that repeatedly until he reaches the top. But if the stranger below chooses not to do so, the journeyer on the bridge will let go of the rope and allow the other to fall. The dangling stranger refuses to pull himself up, so the journeyer lets go of the rope and continues on his journey.

We learn from this fable that responsible leadership or differentiation, whether in families, congregations, and parishes; among friends; or in work systems, is about making responsible decisions and giving other people choices.

Differentiation means staying connected or in relationship while maintaining one's integrity or definition as an individual. To get too close is fusion. It occurs when the forces of "togetherness" become too strong and those in the system lack the maturity to define self apart from the other. The family fights between Mary's two daughters were a sign of fusion or intense emotional interlocking. Two people in fusion are stuck together like wet postage stamps. They are too close and need some distance. When the family is going through transition, fusion or being too close is common. But to become emotionally fused or too close only increases the anxiety and does not encourage emotional maturity. Differentiation means maintaining the integrity of the self while staying connected with others.

To be differentiated, on the other hand, does not mean to cut off or lose connection with others in the family. When people cut off, they become rigid, doctrinaire, judgmental, and inflexible, lacking compassion. When cut-off occurs, the entire system suffers.

Having been terminated from his church, Randy was undergoing transition. He was taking time to evaluate his future, but he was unwilling to get professional help. While in the church, he had been fused with it, allowing it to determine his functioning and identity. After leaving the church, he reacted from the opposite extreme—he began to cut off from friends and family. He spent large periods of time away from the family in the name of work and other obligations. Over time, it became obvious to his wife that he was cutting off. In addition, Randy stopped calling his parents and siblings, to whom he was closely connected, to avoid the questions and the discomfort that the questions raised. But throughout this period, he did not stop to ask about his own contribution to the crises. He focused only on how others had hurt him, blaming them for his termination. He failed to reflect on what he could learn from the experience, or how his functioning might have contributed to the conflict. Randy adopted the role of victim. Anxiety in the family system became more intense until marital conflict rose to a critical level. His wife left him for a time, but the couple eventually entered joint counseling. Randy had to work on his own level of differentiation. He had to ask why he had given the church so much power over him. What had triggered the fusion and the cutoff? How had his functioning contributed to his current plight?

The admonition to work first on self in the system is based on the premise that to help the family most, we must have done our own inner work. Some say, "Isn't that selfish to focus on oneself?" Think about the flight attendant giving safety instructions before the plane takes off: If the plane encounters problems and the oxygen mask drops from above your head, put on your own mask before assisting others with theirs. Unless we take care of ourselves, we can be of no value to those around us whom we love deeply.

Reflect on the following questions. I encourage you to write your responses.

- How do you function within your family system through this time of change? Do you generate, amplify, or lower the anxiety among your family, friends, and colleagues?

- Earlier, we discussed characteristics of differentiation. One of those was the ability to make "I" statements and to take "I" positions. Think about a time when you did take an "I" position in your family, or some other emotional system to which you are connected. What was the effect on others in the system?

- Do you know where you are headed? Do you have a direction, a vision, or a goal? Try to write where you hope to be, your personal and professional goals, for the next five years.

- What are three essential "I believe" statements you can make about life? What are your convictions?

- What are four strengths that you have to offer personally and professionally?

- Think of a time when you reacted without thinking to something said in either your family or work setting. What was the result? Think of another time when you chose to reflect and respond nonanxiously to someone's comment or action. What was the effect on the other person and the system when you responded nonanxiously? What did you do differently in the two responses?

FAMILY OF ORIGIN ISSUES

A second suggestion as we undergo career change and transition from a family systems perspective is to reflect on our family of origin and extended family. Extended family includes grandparents, aunts, uncles, cousins, etc.

Much of the way we deal with anxiety and change we learned from a young age. We learned early on to generate anxiety, to amplify or heighten it, or to lower it by remaining calm or nonanxious. Some of the anxiety we deal with is part of a multigenerational pattern. According to family systems theory, anxiety is transmitted not only from person to person, but also from generation to generation.

To the extent that we can deal with the issues from our childhood nonanxiously, we can deal with current situations proportionately. When we are undergoing change, it is helpful to be aware of the way we learned from our family of origin to deal with anxiety and change. We may need to learn to function in a more healthy and less anxious manner than modeled by our family of origin. If the questions from your childhood are too difficult, I suggest seeing a professional counselor who will work with you on this issue. If finances are a problem, many mental-health clinics offer a sliding fee scale.

In addition, spend time exploring your family tree. This will help you get in touch with the multigenerational issues with which you may be struggling. Try going back at least three generations, tracking births, marriages, deaths, and divorces, as well as traumas and transitions. Look for patterns and motifs.

Reflect on the following questions about family of origin, anxiety, and transition.

- What experiences from your childhood that cause you anxiety and pain have you resisted remembering?

- How did your family of origin deal with change?

- What is your learned anxiety style? Do you generate anxiety in your relationships, do you amplify it, or do you regulate the anxiety, bringing calm to relationship systems?

- How do the ways you function with your family or friends, or in your workplace, reflect what you learned in your family of origin?

- What are personal signs that you are becoming highly anxious?

- How do you deal with anxiety (exercise, art, play, food, argumentativeness)?

- Is there any common issue or motif that keeps surfacing in your family from generation to generation?

- How has your family of origin influenced your vocation of ministry and your ways of relating to others?

- How has your family of origin influenced your way of responding to change and anxiety?

- How can you function differently? What effect would that change have on your family system?

Here are two stories that offer metaphors or images for healthy leadership or differentiation in the family system, including the family of origin, as you undergo change.

First, one way I exercise is by doing karate with my son. In karate, part of the testing involves performing *katas,* a series of moves performed in front of the instructor. At the higher belt levels, the instructor does not count, but you must perform the kata by your own inner count or rhythm. However, from three to five other people are on the floor testing with you, each doing the same kata. The challenge is not to get caught in the tempo of the others on the floor, but to stay with your own inner count, rhythm, and speed. That takes deep concentration and self-definition. As long as I stay with my own inner count and rhythm, I do fine. I get into trouble only when I let the rhythm and speed of others determine mine so that I get pulled out of myself. This example offers an image of the effects of anxiety in the family. It pulls us out of ourselves and tangles us in the anxiety of the family. The anxiety does to us what following another's rhythm and count does to the participants during the kata—it begins to determine our functioning. It draws us into acting and moving in ways that are not healthy for us. The instructor regularly tells students to work at their own speed and to do their own moves. One works only on regulating one's own technique, form, and timing. That is what we need to do in our families when we find anxiety taking over. If we can stay focused on our own presence and functioning and stay calm and nonreactive, our behavior can have a beneficial effect on the family's health and our own.

Edwin Friedman told a story that serves as another metaphor: A jazz band was playing. Some in the group were playing and introducing themselves, while others were listening. At the back of the band was a bass player. As he listened to the others introduce themselves and play their instruments, he noticed that the strings of his instrument began to vibrate. He calmly placed his fingers over the vibrating strings to dampen them.[5] Systemic anxiety does to us what that music did to the instrument; it made the strings start to vibrate and seduced the instrument into sounding. The bass player did not allow the vibration to continue. He did not want his instrument playing until he was ready. We need to let all play their own instruments, while we work on dampening down our own strings. To the level that we as leaders and part of the family system can work on our own presence and functioning, remaining nonanxious, our behavior will have a salutary effect on the family as a system, and other family members will also learn healthy, mature ways to respond to anxiety.

But to the extent that we allow systemic anxiety to determine our functioning, the anxiety will build and symptoms will surface in places and ways we never anticipated. The family is a system or body to which all are connected. Be sensitive to the others, and let your functioning be one of self-definition and healthy connection. To the degree that you can remain calm and nonanxious, the system will do the same and move forward through the transition.

My wife, Martha, my sons, Craig and Blake, our dogs, Max and Muffasa, and I came through our time of change in a healthy way. God brought us to the place where we needed to be. The transition had its time of pain and discomfort, but as we worked to stay connected yet defined, God always showed us a way through the obstacles and gave us the opportunity to grow. Many times I found myself pulled into the anxiety. When I did, Martha would help regulate the anxiety and bring us to a calmer place. When she was pulled into it, I found a way to lower the anxiety. The key was our recognition that we were connected, and thus we were sensitive to one another and to the emotional system in which we live.

Mary, whose story I told at the beginning of this chapter, came through her time of change. She learned about remaining nonanxious or calm. She learned about objectivity in the face of intense anxiety. But looking back, she said it was a time of growth and maturing, and God never let her or her family down.

A Time of Change: Summary of Things to Remember

- *Define self.*
- *Stay connected to others, whether family, friends, or colleagues.*
- *Be aware of how your family of origin handled anxiety.*
- *Respond in a healthy way to anxiety; do not react to it.*
- *Focus on the strengths in the family, not the weaknesses.*
- *Focus on one's own functioning and presence in the family system.*
- *Face conflict; do not avoid or deny it.*
- *Communicate openly with your family members.*
- *Remain open to diversity and difference.*
- *Stay calm and objective in the face of anxious situations.*
- *Pray and trust God through the process.*

How Do We Regulate Anxiety?

To deal with anxiety, these further suggestions may offer help for you, whether married or single, and for your family as you undergo change.

Make time for play with your family and friends. Play is part of healthy spirituality. A symptom of an anxious family system is that members become too serious, lacking playfulness and humor. One way that we bond and stay connected in healthy ways is through play. That can mean going to the park, seeing movies, riding bikes, or playing games. When we were undergoing our transition, our sons reminded us regularly what was most important. While my wife and I had high expectations for the boys and ourselves, the boys reminded us that they did not want much, just to be with us. On New Year's Eve 1999, as the world was planning its party, the boys wanted to play a board game. Play is bonding in a healthy way. If we do not bond through play, other less healthy ways of bonding such as pushing and fighting can surface. Do not underestimate the importance and power of play in times of transition.

Exercise regularly. Exercise is a good way to relieve stress and help us deal with anxiety. As many know, there is a growing awareness of the connection between body and soul. Contemporary thought is moving away from the concept of a split or dichotomy between body and soul. As a system, what affects one affects the other. In fact, body and mind or soul can be imaged not as separate entities but as different sides of the entity.

The point is that the way one treats one's body is important to the health of the whole. In transition we need to be especially mindful of our physical, emotional, and spiritual health.

Listen to music. Both listening to music and making your own is relaxing and reduces anxiety.

Tend to art and creativity. To nurture the inner life, some creative expression is helpful during transition to reduce anxiety and to listen to your inner self.

Sign up for a class, creating a new interest or nurturing an old one. Focusing our interest and our creative energies is an excellent tool to relieve anxiety.

Pray. Spend time in silence and prayer about your situation and decisions.

Read. I often read something unrelated to my current situation to give me an outlet and a broader perspective on life.

Clean your house or apartment. When under stress or anxiety, my wife cleans house. She says that cleaning house brings order and reduces anxiety.

Plant or work in a garden. Working with our hands in the soil is therapeutic. In the monastic tradition, working in the soil is part of the spiritual discipline.

Keep a journal. One person called journals "the poor person's therapist." I talked to a minister who was going through a career change. I asked if he was keeping a journal. He had not thought of it, but decided it was an excellent idea for his learning and growth. Since then, he has told me that writing has been a gift.

Make the anxiety you feel into a research project. Ask yourself questions like, "What is there in me or my past that is creating this kind of response?" "How can I respond differently?" Making oneself a student of one's situation is a learning experience, offering meaning and purpose, and reducing anxiety.

Spend time talking to family members and extended family to learn about your past. Make a family tree to bring new insights.

Encourage or lend someone a helping hand.

Volunteer for services in the community.

Take time to breathe deeply, slowly.

Keep your daily routine, remembering that your feelings come and go.

Care for and play with your pets.

Stay in contact with your friends. As one ponders important decisions, friends are helpful in allowing us to think freely and in challenging our perspectives.

Keep healthy and regular eating and rest habits. Get plenty of rest, and eat balanced meals. Transition often takes more emotional energy than we realize. I am diabetic, and as stress and anxiety rise, my eating habits become more critical to regulating my blood sugar.

If you or your family is having trouble with the transition, invest in a spiritual director, therapist, or pastoral counselor. Many pastoral counselors charge on a sliding scale, so lack of money does not have to be a barrier. Open communication and tending to the needs of those in the family system are important. As a physician is needed when our child is sick, sometimes an outside resource is needed when the family system experiences anxiety and change.

Get a physical examination, and stay in touch with your physician.

As you enter this time of transition or at least the stage of considering it, if you have the luxury, make certain your finances are in order and organized. Formulate a family budget to make it through the transition. In working with the budget, bring others in on the process at the level they need to know. By "need to know," I mean that it is not necessary to inform a child of all aspects, but to give him or her the general picture that the family is on a fixed income. This knowledge can help children grow through the process, regulate their own spending, and feel that they are contributing.

Formulate your vision and write a plan for it. If you are married and have children, share your vision with family members and let them share their vision with you. I would suggest a vision for a five-year and a ten-year plan for your life. If you are married, it is important for others in your family system to participate. For you to see their vision is important as well. Having a direction in life is healthy for any person, especially during times of transition, giving everyone a common goal. Goals offer direction and lower anxiety. They assist the immune system within the family system when it is undergoing vulnerable times like a career transition.

Throughout the transition, try to focus on the positive. An old hymn uses the phrase "Count your blessings." The outcome of a transition has much to do with the way we perceive it. Emotionally, when I can see the positive in the transition, that view has an energizing effect on those undergoing the change. This does not mean that we cannot express negative feelings and experiences, but it does mean balance. We do not want to get stuck in the negative.

Transitions take time. If you are undergoing a transition now, remind yourself that it will not last forever. You can grow through this interval, and one day you will look back, as we did, and see how you learned from it. In the meantime, attend the unattended moment.

If you are married and have children, try to affirm yourself, your spouse, and your children periodically. If you are single, try to affirm yourself and affirm a friend. Affirmation needs to be authentic, but often we take each other for granted. We tell others when they do wrong, but we forget to tell them that we appreciate their support and positive attitude through the transition. When anxiety rises, the negative diagnosis of others increases. Stay away from that reactive position, and try to affirm and encourage others. Talk around the dinner table about the transition, hear others' feelings and experiences, and voice your own. Affirmation from those we love creates a healthy atmosphere and goes a long way in helping self-esteem and supportive systems.

Write letters to old friends and family members. This activity symbolizes connecting to our past.

As you undergo a time of change that creates anxiety, add to the list. It may help you, and it may also be a gift to someone else who can learn from your experience.

Embrace the Challenge

My final statement about looking at a time of change from a systems perspective is that it can be a wonderful time to embrace challenge and grow. Be sensitive to transition, for it gives us the greatest opportunity for healthy change. A paradoxical statement as you think systemically about your situation is, "There is always more going on than what meets the eye. In fact, that which meets the eye is the very thing that is probably not going on." Peace and grace be with you as you consider and move through transition. If you stay on the journey, the words of T. S. Eliot best describe my experience of the journey, and I believe they will yours. He writes:

I said to my soul, be still, and let the dark come upon you
Which shall be the darkness of God . . .

I said to my soul, be still, and wait without hope
For hope would be hope for the wrong thing; wait without love
For love would be love of the wrong thing; there is yet faith
But the faith and the love and the hope are all in the waiting.
Wait without thought, for you are not ready for thought:
So the darkness shall be the light, and the stillness the Dancing.[6]

As you continue on your journey, listen for God's voice. Darkness and stillness will be part of the journey. But the darkness will become light, the stillness the dancing.

CHAPTER 4

Surviving the Change

Every minister I know is a survivor. You have survived parish politics, difficult people, and the loss of your idealistic views of what ministry is and what ministers do. Each of us has a choice about how we tell our own story. We can talk about the difficulties we have faced and the damage that being in ministry has caused us or our family. We can also tell the story of the internal resources we have acquired through our efforts to remain contributing clergy, given the challenges of professional ministry. These internal resources will continue to serve you well if you choose to remain in ministry. If you are leaving professional ministry, you have gifts and skills to take with you on the journey. This chapter will aid you in recalling and using your survival skills.

PERSONAL STRATEGIES FOR TRANSITION SURVIVAL

Have you noticed that some people can repeatedly face complex challenges and remain calm and emotionally centered, perhaps even flourishing? Have you wondered how that was possible? I believe surviving well is a skill that consists of discrete strategies, ones that can be learned. Some of these skills are useful for navigating any type of transition. I offer you ten strategies.

1. REMEMBER WHO YOU ARE

It is easy to lose yourself so that your personhood and your profession become fused. You know the ministers whose entire identities are tied up in being "Pastor So-and-So." When they are asked to step out of the pastoral role, it is as if they don't know themselves. We all know people who are so enmeshed with family, job, addiction, or self that they no longer know who they are. This enmeshment seems to be particularly common among clergy. As women continue to enter pastoral ministry, we'll see examples of this condition more often among female clergy.

Remembering who you are is called in psychological theory "differentiation." *The Dictionary of Pastoral Care and Counseling* defines individuation (for which differentiation is a synonym) as "a process of differentiation having as a goal the development of a conscious, complete, unique, individual personality capable of successful social as well as inner relationship."[1]

Have you ever uttered statements like "Every single member of my church is my boss"? This statement suggests that the minister may not have a well-defined self. Every member can be a boss only if you, the minister, have lost your sense of your internal authority.

Remembering who you truly are begins with your personhood, not your profession. To reinforce your sense of personal self, write below five personal qualities you like about yourself. Beside each quality, write one example of how you have recently used this personal quality. Examples of personal qualities are sense of humor, integrity, faithfulness, loyalty.

1. _____

2. _____

3. _____

4. _____

5. _____

How easy was it for you to recall five personal qualities? I believe the beginning point of surviving change is to distinguish between your professional self and your personal self.

My observation is that outside factors strongly influence who a pastor is as a person, how a pastor acts as a person, and what priorities a pastor sets as a person. For example, pastors often let the denomination define not only their ministry, but also their personhood.

Which outside influences have most strongly affected your personhood? Please list. Examples are family of origin, spouse, and denominational expectations.

- _____
- _____
- _____
- _____
- _____
- _____

To which of these influences do you want to continue paying attention? Which ones do you want to let go of? Whether you are staying in professional ministry or leaving, knowing who you are and remaining clearly defined as a person is a core skill to acquire. This skill is called being "differentiated" by the Murray Bowen school of family-systems therapy. An illustration of the concept: You are in your boat by yourself. While others (spouse, parents, denominational leaders) may pull their boats next to yours, they remain in their own boats. Differentiated people do not fuse together so that they think, act, and feel alike; they stay in their own boats.

2. DEVELOP THE SKILL OF MATURE DEPENDENCY

None of us is an island unto ourselves (at least if we're healthy). John Donne was right about that. Rather, emotionally healthy people learn how to depend appropriately on others. This is how I define mature dependency. Appropriate dependence means being aware of your need for outside support and being willing to call on others for support without becoming dependent on them.

Appropriate dependence also means learning how to tell who is dependable. In a church, learning which individuals and groups are dependable and trustworthy is often confusing and difficult. Let me illustrate. Pastor Jones was recently called to a new parish. On the day she and her family moved into the rectory no one worked harder than the chair of the search committee. Learning the community, meeting individuals in the parish, and meeting civic leaders was no problem. The chair of the search committee made it happen.

Simultaneously, this committee chair was suggesting ways the pastor could improve her liturgy, preaching, pastoral care, and leadership. Pastor Jones thought she couldn't do anything correctly. She was learning that the search committee chair was so interested in her success that he was stifling her creativity and pastoral influence. Having a relationship of mature dependence with him was unlikely, because he was too highly invested in the pastor's success. He had climbed into the pastor's boat!

People with whom we can have a relationship of mature dependency are people who will see us and accept us as we are and at the same time give us objective feedback. Relationships of mature dependence can aid us in facing enormous challenges without crashing and burning.

List below those with whom you have a relationship of mature dependency.

- _____
- _____
- _____
- _____
- _____

Have you called on any of them for assistance?

3. TURN INSIGHT INTO ACTION

Insight brought about by the courageous searching of one's past and present life and one's family of origin and family of choice can be of great value to you. However, it can be of profound value only if you turn your insight into action.

Since we are not passive objects, we can choose a new action. Consider the story of Lew, a middle-aged Presbyterian pastor. Because of his lack of confidence, he allowed his profile to be mailed only to a narrow range of congregations. Lew entered pastoral counseling and over a period of time heard his mother's voice ringing in his ears: "Lew, you're the dumbest kid I've got!" As he continued in counseling, Lew recognized that his mother was incorrect. Lew is intellectually gifted and a joy to be with as pastor and friend.

This new insight (that his mother was wrong) ultimately led to new behavior. Lew began being open to churches he would not have considered before his insight was worked through.

Mary had a successful first career in the banking industry. She was also a faithful church member serving on the church council and chairing the finance committee. Increasingly her thoughts turned to seminary and a second career as a minister. Over time she made plans to leave her job, go to seminary, and pursue her dream.

Mary was an outstanding student. Not only did she have a straight-A academic average; she also won the seminary's outstanding preaching award in her senior year.

Six months after graduation Mary was called to a church that averaged 50 to 65 worshippers on Sunday. Mary's dream had come true.

Mary's dream soon turned to a nightmare. The part-time church secretary who had "held the church together" during the interim began competing with Mary for the role of pastor. Congregational leaders, not wanting to confront the secretary, gave Mary no support.

Within 24 months Mary had left local-church ministry for a role dealing with denominational finances. She continues to serve as a supply preacher at area churches. Mary is fortunate. Many ministers would simply have left professional ministry altogether, never to return.

If you are feeling stuck, the American Association of Pastoral Counselors can often help you find a pastoral counselor near your area. Call 703-385-6967 for specific names and contact information. Spiritual Directors

International can also provide you with a list of spiritual directors (call 415-566-1560, or write to 1329 Seventh Ave., San Francisco CA 94122-2507). Many also find bibliotherapy (the use of books to help produce insight) helpful. Since new books are constantly being published, I'd suggest you check your local library or bookstore for resources under both the self-help and business/career headings.

Like Lew and Mary, you may have found yourself significantly affected by someone else's story about you. Below, write a story about a time you achieved the insight "This problem in living isn't about me, the problem is about my _____." or "This problem in living is about me and I can choose a new behavior." Perhaps you are achieving the insight you've been needing right now.

If you are feeling stuck now and needing new insight, use your skill of mature dependency and reach out to others. Maybe you will reach out to a friend, perhaps to a professional, or possibly both.

4. Be an Artistic Inventor

The past two years of my life have demanded the highest degree of professional creativity I've ever had to call on. Within 18 months after beginning a new job, I found myself feeling near the edge of burnout. After speaking about these feelings with my spiritual director, I decided to try two new behaviors.

First, I joined a church-league volleyball team with my teenage daughter, Lauren. We had a good time being together. She's on her high school's varsity volleyball team, and she quickly became my teacher. I was getting something for myself, time with Lauren, and a new sports skill. I'm a better Dad than volleyball player, but it was fun, and the burned-out feeling was going away.

The second thing I tried was pottery lessons, given to me by my family for last year's birthday; I'd been too busy to use my gift! For eight weeks I was a potter. The first time I threw a pot on a pottery wheel I exclaimed, "It's the best pot I've ever made!" This new creative outlet was great fun, relaxing, and life giving.

Why tell you these personal stories? I want to stress that losing and reclaiming the artist within are normal occurrences. In times of great stress or transition, you and I often misplace the creative side of ourselves. I would also emphasize that nurturing personal creativity in one arena of life is a good way to keep channels open for discovering creative solutions in other arenas. Being an artistic inventor can also give you a way to channel the energy of your pain rather than exploding internally or externally.

Living well through conflict or transition requires imagination. Remembering to play as a way to achieve emotional repair and remembering to be an artistic inventor as a way to channel your pain can be critical to surviving well, whether you are trying to stay in professional ministry with the least damage possible or looking to make a transition out of ministry with a minimum of harm.

List below the play or artistic activities that you are willing to investigate. Heed your visceral reactions without allowing your rational self to censor what you most want to try. Locate one resource for each activity you list (for example, a dance studio or potter who teaches lessons in your area), and write it and a phone number by each activity. Finally, designate the date by which you will make an initial exploration. An example might be:

- *Cajun dancing*   *UNO*   *333-4567*   *June 15*
- _____
- _____
- _____
- _____
- _____

Did you list anything? You are too important not to play and invent. What would you love to learn to do?

5. KEEP YOUR SENSE OF HUMOR.

Laughter makes a heart merry. Humor has the capacity both to reduce a problem to its actual size and to make you large enough to face the problem. Humor is another way of being an artistic inventor.

The modern study of humor began in 1905 with Sigmund Freud's publication of *Jokes and Their Relation to the Unconscious*. In psychoanalytic theory, humor gives us pleasure in two ways. *First*, in the frivolous, illogical associations of the comic, we are given an opportunity to release tension built up in our overrational, demanding world. The nonsense of humor permits regression to childish ways of thinking and behaving. Second, humor may release inhibited fantasies (e.g., sexual or aggressive), which would otherwise be banned from conscious recognition and public communication. Humor, like the dream, is a camouflage that momentarily deceives the superego, as unacceptable impulses are allowed expression in a socially acceptable manner. From this perspective, humor may be compared to art, play, and games. These are socially acceptable and creative channels of liberation from constraints of logic, language, and proper conduct.

Some have suggested that faith and humor are linked in that both demonstrate a capacity to transcend oneself. One thing is sure—humor is fundamental to our well-being. Writer and magazine editor Norman Cousins documented in *Anatomy of an Illness* how he hastened his recovery from a dangerous disease by watching Marx Brothers films and reruns of "Candid Camera."

There is one television show I make every effort to see weekly. Might it be PBS or something on the Learning Channel? No, it's "Third Rock from the Sun," a sitcom about aliens in the bodies of humans who are attempting to learn the social mores of humans. Why do I watch it? Because it makes me laugh. Below identify something that makes you laugh.

6. ENGAGE IN RECREATION

Recreation is time to refresh oneself physically, mentally, and spiritually. I need this skill. I've done better at playing and being an artistic inventor than I've done at regular recreation. I even laugh often. However, recreation takes time.

Below list the last three times you took enough time away from your work and everyday routine to refresh yourself physically and mentally.

- _____
- _____
- _____

When you do take time for recreation, what are the activities and attitudes you need to leave behind? List below:

- _____
- _____
- _____

Do you have time scheduled to recreate? If so, describe it below. If not, write below a plan with dates and places to begin re-creating yourself. Many monasteries offer reasonable accommodations where body, mind, and spirit can experience renewal.

7. STAY ANCHORED IN YOUR VALUES

Knowing your values is knowing what really matters to you in life. The following process designed by the late Joseph Fabry, a pioneer in the field of logotherapy, will help you clarify your values. (Logotherapy is a counseling theory that emphasizes finding meaning in any circumstance in which you find yourself.)

Part 1: List of Values

Below is a list of 20 values. Read it and mark the five items you think are most important to you and the five you think are least important to you. (This list is from the work of the logotherapist James C. Crumbaugh, *Logotherapy—New Help for Problem Drinkers* [Chicago: Nelson-Hall, 1981], 107).

1.   to be wealthy
2.   to have lasting friendships
3.   to have physical sex
4.   to have a good name
5.   to be remembered favorably after death
6.   to gain romantic love
7.   to be a great leader of people
8.   to be healthy
9.   to be a hero or heroine
10. to be of great service to people
11. to be famous
12. to be physically powerful (men) beautiful (women)
13. to be an intellectual genius
14. to find adventure and new experiences
15. to be happy
16. to understand the mystery of life
17. to fulfill religious goals
18. to have peace of mind
19. to gain social acceptance and belonging
20. to gain a personal identity

Part 2: Your Value Hierarchy[2]

On pages 82 and 83 you will find a selection sheet. The numbers on that sheet refer to the values in Part 1 (1 = to be wealthy, 2 = to have lasting friendships, and so on). The columns on the selection sheet allow you to compare each value with every other value. In each pair listed, circle the value you consider the higher of the two.

For example, in the first column the first line asks you to choose between 1 and 2, between wealth and friendship. If you consider being wealthy more important than having lasting friendships, circle the 1; if friendship is more important, circle the 2. Make this comparison and choice with every pair in all columns. The column becomes shorter because values have been compared in previous columns. The last column consists of only one pair (19—to gain social acceptance and belonging, versus 20—to gain a personal identity).

Now go over the entire list, add all the circled 1's, and enter the total in the box under the first column. In this instance you will find all circled 1's in the first column. For the rest of the values, you will find a single column of comparisons plus one comparison in each of the previous columns. Add up all the circled numbers and enter the total in the box under that value (indicating how much you value the item). When you get to the last column, you will have to go through all the previous columns to find all the other 20s you have circled. When you have done that, enter the total under column 20.

Look at the numbers in the 20 boxes on the selection sheet on pages 82 and 83. They show your value hierarchy. How does this compare with your off-the-cuff estimate in part 1? What surprises you in this evaluation? What are the five highest and five lowest values in part 2? Do they match your evaluation from part 1? Does your hierarchy give you any insight into yourself? Is there anything you would want to change? What would you have to change in your lifestyle to reflect a change in your value hierarchy? Are you prepared to make this change, or are you satisfied with your present lifestyle and habits? Each of the following questions can be used to start a dialogue with yourself.

- How do I feel about my values?
- What implications do my values have for my personal life?
- What implications do my values have for my professional life?

Knowing and living by your values will help you stay anchored during a period of questioning or transition.

SELECTION SHEET

1-2	2-3	3-4	4-5	5-6	6-7	7-8	8-9	9-10	10-11
1-3	2-4	3-5	4-6	5-7	6-8	7-9	8-10	9-11	10-12
1-4	2-5	3-6	4-7	5-8	6-9	7-10	8-11	9-12	10-13
1-5	2-6	3-7	4-8	5-9	6-10	7-11	8-12	9-13	10-14
1-6	2-7	3-8	4-9	5-10	6-11	7-12	8-13	9-14	10-15
1-7	2-8	3-9	4-10	5-11	6-12	7-13	8-14	9-15	10-16
1-8	2-9	3-10	4-11	5-12	6-13	7-14	8-15	9-16	10-17
1-9	2-10	3-11	4-12	5-13	6-14	7-15	8-16	9-17	10-18
1-10	2-11	3-12	4-13	5-14	6-15	7-16	8-17	9-18	10-19
1-11	2-12	3-13	4-14	5-15	6-16	7-17	8-18	9-19	10-20
1-12	2-13	3-14	4-15	5-16	6-17	7-18	8-19	9-20	
1-13	2-14	3-15	4-16	5-17	6-18	7-19	8-20		
1-14	2-15	3-16	4-17	5-18	6-19	7-20			
1-15	2-16	3-17	4-18	5-19	6-20				
1-16	2-17	3-18	4-19	5-20					
1-17	2-18	3-19	4-20						
1-18	2-19	3-20							
1-19	2-20								
1-20									

11-12	12-13	13-14	14-15	15-16	16-17	17-18	18-19	19-20
11-13	12-14	13-15	14-16	15-17	16-18	17-19	18-20	
11-14	12-15	13-16	14-17	15-18	16-19	17-20		
11-15	12-16	13-17	14-18	15-19	16-20			
11-16	12-17	13-18	14-19	15-20				
11-17	12-18	13-19	14-20					
11-18	12-19	13-20						
11-19	12-20							
11-20								

8. Maintain Your Health

One of the greatest gifts we possess is our health. In a transition period, health needs to be maintained; perhaps you can even improve your health. Healthy eating habits, regular exercise, regular physical exams, and healthy thoughts make for good health. There will be many things regarding your health you can't control (regardless of what others say). But you can be in control of the habits that lead to good health.

Name one action that you are willing to take this week to begin taking control of your health. Some suggestions might be:

- I'll begin getting an adequate amount of sleep nightly.
- I'll schedule a physical exam this week.
- I'll begin walking 20 minutes daily.

9. Remember: You Have Choices and Can Take Action

You choose whether you will tell your story as if you are a survivor or a victim. You can also choose to move yourself out of the victim role, if that is the one you have been playing.

What three actions, in any areas of your life, do you need to take now to improve your chances not only to survive but also to thrive in life? The other eight strategies in this section will likely give you some clues.

1.

2.

3.

Professional Strategies for Transition Survival

1. Consider a Career Assessment

Career assessment is a significant period of time set aside for reflection on your career. The career assessment normally lasts a total of two to three days and in a few cases up to five days. Some are done on consecutive days; other career assessments may be spread over several weekend days or entire weekends.

Many career assessments involve taking several psychological and vocational tests before the assessment begins. They will be scored and interpreted by professionals qualified to do so. The data are then used in the career assessment. Some of the most common instruments used are:

1. The Myers-Briggs Type Indicator, a personality-type indicator using four scales. The most widely known scale is the introversion-extroversion scale.

2. The Minnesota Multiphasic Personality Indicator is a psychological tool that gives an in-depth look at one's personality traits. The MMPI must be scored and interpreted by a professionally trained mental-health worker who is certified or licensed by the state.

3. The Fundamental Interpersonal Relationship Orientation-Behavior (FIRO-B) is a tool that helps an individual better understand how he or she most often relates to groups of people.

4. The Strong Vocational Inventory measures your vocational interests against people in 124 occupation scales and six general occupational themes. The Strong Vocational measures how similar the person tested is to the people in various occupations. The theory behind the instrument is that the more you are like people in your vocation, the more satisfaction you'll feel with the career. This instrument is an interest, not an aptitude, instrument.

5. An aptitude test may also be administered. There are a great many aptitude tests available to career counselors. The aptitude instrument can help you see where your abilities and your interests match.

Once your battery of tests has been completed, the career assessment will help you explore areas such as:

1. *Your calling.* This gift from God that can transform a minister's life has been explored in some depth in chapter 2. You may want to refer to pages 23-50.

2. *Fulfillment.* Fulfillment refers generally to how much joy there is in your work. Fulfillment refers specifically to the question, "From what areas of your work does the most joy spring?"

3. *Skills.* You may be asked to list several accomplishments of which you are especially proud. Then you may be asked to discover the skills used to achieve your accomplishment. This discovery process will be guided by your career counselor.

You'll likely explore other issues such as, "What is your support system like, and who is in it?" You'll also delineate a plan for yourself about how to continue this work of discovery and growth. I believe doing a career assessment is the most helpful place to start when you are considering a professional transition.

Many judicatories retain a career-counseling service to be available to their clergy. For information on what career-counseling services are available in your area, you might start with your judicatory office.

2. TRY NOT TO LEAVE YOUR POSITION UNTIL YOU HAVE SOMEWHERE TO GO

My experience has been that clergy who leave the church without somewhere to go regret the decision because the resulting financial burden compounds all other issues. They often feel relief if they have been in a cauldron of conflict. That is, they feel relief until the realization hits: "My God, what have I done? I have a family to support!" More pragmatically, it is often more difficult to move to a new professional ministry position if you are unemployed.

Some clergy will not have a choice as to whether or not they leave. These clergy will be terminated. A few clergy (compared to all the clergy fired) have betrayed the trust of an individual and a congregation by sexual or other acts. The family can be left without a parent, the spouse without a mate. The church family is left without a pastor. The pastor is left needing help and without a basic unit of support or a career. The loss can be enormous.

Most clergy are fired because they get caught up in a conflict left simmering from generations before. The pot simply boils over, scalding the pastor and the pastor's family, leaving lifelong scars, if the wounds ever heal at all. This should not be. Often judicatories will have small stipends, insurance coverage for a specified time period, pastoral counselors, or other mental-health professionals contracted to provide counseling or other services for terminated clergy and their families. Your willingness to ask for help will be a source of hope to you and, if applicable, your family.

If at all possible (and it may not be), don't leave before you have somewhere to go.

3. CONSIDER NOT GOING FAR

There are two types of career moves. One is to move to a moderately different career. This move might be from parish minister to hospice chaplain. In this move you can use the skills and education you have already acquired with little or no retraining. You can move vocationally without going far.

Becoming an administrator within a not-for-profit community agency might be another way to move and not go far. The same administrative skills you used to direct the work of a parish are used in a community agency. If you were an ineffective administrator as a pastor, however, would the above move be a solid choice? Probably not.

A friend of mine is the most engaging preacher I know. Choosing to leave ministry, he chose a new career working as a motivational speaker for a company that helps congregations raise building funds. He moved without going far. He loves the travel, meeting each new congregation and speaking to their unique challenges.

Get the point? First, determine your most effective skills in ministry, then see if you can use those same skills in a different arena.

The second type of move is to a radically different career. This move might take you to a different context, such as from a not-for-profit organization to a for-profit organization. Such a move might take you to a context in which business, not ministry, is the primary, or only, emphasis. This move might also require new skills. I believe all radical career moves require new training.

For example, in my field of pastoral counseling, most states today require a person to be licensed or certified by the state to become a counselor. Most master's-level counseling degrees are designed as two years of study. After the degree is granted, roughly two years of internship are required before a person can practice mental health counseling without supervision. A career move requiring four years of retraining is a radical move. Not impossible, but very ambitious.

Evaluating what type of career move you both want to make and can afford to make is important for all clergy.

4. TALK TO PEOPLE IN OTHER PROFESSIONS

Once you locate a profession you have interest in, find someone in that field who will let you shadow their day and allow you to ask pertinent questions such as:

1. Are you fulfilled in your career? What do you like about it? What challenges you?
2. What training or education must one have for this job?
3. What is the career outlook for this job? (The Occupational Outlook Handbook found in the reference section of public libraries can help you with this question.)
4. What is the salary range for this occupation in this section of the country?
5. You'll have a thousand more excellent questions.

When you decide what career area you are going to pursue, be on the lookout for a mentor. This person can help you make up time you lost in your new profession while you were in ministry. If you decide to stay in ministry, a mentor is an equally valuable companion to have.

5. BE PATIENT

I am convinced, although I have no scientific data behind me, that it takes from five to seven years to reestablish oneself after major personal, family, or career tumult. You've already read my narrative in chapter 2. After leaving my job on a national church level, because of an act of conscience, regaining my footing in a new career and in my adopted denomination took seven years. I believe this was within a normative time range.

What are the tasks in this five-to-seven-year time span? I believe there are three major tasks:

Grieve. Grief is a process that many researchers and writers have described. I found myself grief-stricken for a full two years after I left my national church post. I felt betrayed by those who had taken over my denomination. I felt angry; this event was unjust. Mostly I felt sad and afraid—sad as I watched dozens of friends being metaphorically murdered in the name of orthodoxy; afraid because my career world was crumbling around me.

Explore. Exploring new career options both inside and outside ministry takes patience. Earlier in the chapter, what I didn't say about survival skills is that they are beginning points, not the end. Once you've completed a career assessment, you'll revisit the results for months afterward on a regular basis. The same is true for all the other skills. Each is a building block rather than a completed house.

Act. Finally, you must act. Even inaction is passive activity. In my experience, acting is both courageous and scary. Although it may feel less risky not to act, those who are too afraid to risk will lose valuable time and perhaps even a part of themselves.

Throughout all these skills you will likely need to call on outside help. Remember, the more emotionally healthy you are, the sooner you can reach out for help. Do it now!

SPIRITUAL STRATEGIES FOR TRANSITION SURVIVAL

The vast majority of this book's readers have framed their lives around the God of Abraham, Sarah, and Jesus. Now you may be at a crossroads where you are deciding whether ministry is professionally where you choose to spend your life. Below are some spiritual strategies to help you through this time.

1. ADMIT TO YOURSELF AND TO GOD HOW YOU FEEL TOWARD GOD

Many of you have come to this fork in the road because of how people who claim to be God's people, and churches that claim to be Christian churches, have treated you and your family. I know you can be hurt deeply because I have been hurt deeply.

How do you feel toward God? You may be angry, feeling that God has let you down. "Where were you, God, when those folks were hurting me, my spouse, my children?" You may have ten different ways you feel toward God. I believe it is important to say how you feel aloud to God, even if you have to yell it!

It may or may not be safe to tell a small group in your church (who may have made your life miserable) or your ministerial colleagues how you feel. It is safe to tell God both how you feel toward God and how you feel toward those people.

Not only is it safe; it's healing. You may want a trusted friend or your spiritual director to be with you. You may want a pastoral counselor to be with you. You may shout it out, write it out, sing it out, or beat it out (pillows, please, with a counselor!). Getting the feelings out in your own way is important.

2. RECOGNIZE YOUR FAITH AND YOUR CAREER AS SEPARATE ENTITIES

My grandmother used to say, "Don't throw the baby out with the bathwater." Of course this is a metaphor about saving what is good and can be saved even if the good is awash in that which is dirty.

If you can manage it, don't throw out your personal faith or your relationship with the holy catholic church because the members of Bayou Self Church are meaner than snakes! I'm convinced that sometimes you have to throw it out, at least until you regain your balance. I also believe God understands why you might need to, at least for a season.

I also believe making your personal faith and your career in ministry synonymous is dangerous. Here's why: Earlier in the chapter I wrote about the concept of individuation. I defined is as "a process of differentiation having as its goal the development of a conscious, complete, unique, individual personality . . ." In other words: who you are (including your faith) is not who your church is, how church members are treating you, or how many folks are showing up on Sunday morning. Stay individuated!

Keeping your faith separate from your career will likely be helpful to you in deciding which fork in the road is best to take now.

3. APPROACH SPIRITUAL DISCIPLINES IN A WAY HELPFUL FOR YOU

Most of us have predominant styles. I think of the styles as thinking, feeling, acting. The spiritual disciplines are broad enough in variety to help you find a way to live the spiritual life that feels right for you. All three styles are equally valuable. Below are several examples of what I mean.

Thinking. Bible study is often a thinking exercise. The Sunday school movement, weekday Bible study groups, and individual biblical study can be aimed at "What did you learn from this passage of Scripture?" Ministers are familiar with this thinking style because of preaching sermons or preparing to teach. As a spiritual discipline, biblical study is different. Biblical study as a spiritual discipline is a way of listening to both God's word and to God. Thinkers study as their way to listen to God.

Feeling. Feelers expect to feel God's presence. Through meditation or a journal or music, feelers both talk to God and listen for God.

Meditation is often used as a spiritual discipline to allow yourself to reverse a loss of feelings. Therein is the paradox; as one lets go of the day and its activity, in the void is God. One feels God's presence as one turns loose of today.

Keeping a journal is a way of remembering the day's activity and how one felt about the day. As a spiritual discipline, writing in a journal is a way of remembering where God has been present and absent today and how one feels about the day's events, as well as God's presence or absence.

Music is a common way of feeling God's presence and absence. "Sometimes I Feel Like a Motherless Child" is more than a great spiritual. Sometimes the spiritual's title is my testimony. In the same way, I have sometimes heard G. F. Handel's "I Know that My Redeemer Liveth" and have felt more hopeful. Music helps me feel both God's presence and absence.

Acting. For some, acting out their spirituality is a way of experiencing God's presence. Seeing where God is at work in the world and joining with God in that work is some people's primary style of spirituality. Seeking peace and justice for all people, serving the underserved, and being God's hands in the world are important to the action-oriented.

Perhaps seeking a balance of thinking, feeling, and acting spiritually is what we all do.

4. Consider (Again) Working with a Spiritual Director

The importance of having a spiritual companion has been discussed (see pages 45 and 46). I have to give the idea one more push. In times of transition, having someone to listen with me for God has been especially important. Perhaps my ears were filled with anxiety or fear about the unknown. What I do know is that a spiritual director, through her presence and our dialogue, has heard God before I did. For me, my relationship with my director and listening for God together was where grace met grace. I hope for you the same gift.

GRACE LURKS

Surviving change is hard. Yet, grace is lurking in the ordinary events of this extraordinary time. New insights leading to new actions become a cause to celebrate. Creative activities lost as you moved up the ladder are now joyfully found again. Values are reestablished, leading to a new sense of personal identity. Yes, grace is lurking.

Perhaps the psalmist wrote what you are feeling, at least some of the time:

I will sing to the Lord
For He has dealt with me richly (Psalm 13:6a, CEV).

CHAPTER 5

Can I Find Myself Again
after Leaving the Ministry?

I am making several assumptions as I begin this chapter. First, if you are still reading this book and engaged with it, you are serious about reinventing yourself. This reinvention may involve staying where you now minister, but with a new attitude. It may mean adding new skills to those you already possess. Or you may have decided your reinvention will be more radical—perhaps you'll embark on a new role, a new career, or a new location.

I am also assuming that if you have read the book this far and completed the written exercises, you have already recognized that with every gain there is a loss. When you set about to reinvent yourself professionally, you are making changes of a magnitude I would call systemic. When you reinvent yourself vocationally, every social system in which you are involved (family, work, educational, religious, and so forth) is affected. One task of adulthood is to stay deeply connected to these social systems without being so stuck in them we are not clear where the social system ends and we as individuals begin. One sign of a person's emotional health is the ability to love and to work. Yet it is unhealthy to feel that one's love is so deep one must stay. You have heard someone say, "I could never leave them even though I know they hurt me. I love them too much." This abused person can't imagine himself or herself without the abuser. When you see yourself as a separate being with needs and wants and can also be emotionally invested in love and work, this is called being "differentiated" as discussed in a previous chapter.

As you successfully individuate from social systems, you can begin the journey of reinventing yourself. How will you know when you are individuated? When your worth as a person no longer depends on how many people were in worship last Sunday, that is one good sign.

During this reinvention time you will clearly see the gains and losses you experience. You may also look at human and career development in a new way. While you might view career development as a matter of growth and improvement up to adulthood, stability in middle age and decline in old age, in this chapter you'll discover your capacity to grow throughout your career while being aware of the career developmental stage you are in.

You'll be able to see that people, including yourself, can be adaptable throughout their life span. Developing your career is a lifelong process that you can shape. In this chapter you'll see a panoramic view of career development. You'll be able to reflect on what you've lost, what has remained the same, and what you've gained because of choosing your career path. You'll also be able to conceptualize the successful reinvention of yourself professionally. We are using the term *reinventing* as a metaphor to speak about successful job transition. First, let's take a look at the process of proactive career development.

The process of career clarification, even for clergy, is a normal part of continuing to grow. Who I am at 50 years of age is not who I was in my 20s. Over those years my ideas about professional ministry have expanded, for at least two reasons.

First, my knowledge of ministerial roles has broadened. At age 20 I would have never thought being an author could be a ministerial role. Today I know many authors and editors who use their gifts and skills in the service of the church. Second, in the past 30 years I have become open to a variety of professional ministerial roles. At 20 I believed if a person was called to professional ministry, he (and it would always be a man) would be the pastor of a church. Now I see dozens of career choices for those called to professional ministry, both male and female.

For me the confusion has never been "Am I supposed to be in professional ministry?" Rather, it has concerned my preferred role in professional ministry. Many of my seminary friends have had other experiences. Their search has led them to question whether they are best suited for the professional minister's role or another calling among the priesthood of all believers. After walking with several friends through this time of discernment, I believe the theological move from "once a priest, always a priest" to "the priesthood of all believers" is far longer than it was ever intended to be. Priests and pastors are already members of the priesthood of all believers.

The paragraph above shows a normal process. One hopes that none of us ends up exactly where we started in any area of our life, including our vocational life. Perhaps as you read this you are feeling as though it is wrong to question your calling or your role in professional ministry. Sometimes our family, our church, or we ourselves decide we should not question matters of faith. If you are feeling this, I want you to know I am convinced your questions and explorations are natural. The questions you raise now and work through effectively will make you a stronger, more effective minister, whether in the church as a professional minister or in the church as an active church member. The danger is to know you need to do this searching and fail to do it. Whenever we ignore or deny a natural process out of a concern for shoulds and oughts, we are asking for trouble.

The process of career clarification is also developmental. After 20 years of doing career counseling with clergy, I am convinced that the first five years after seminary are the hardest. During this early career time a minister is asking the question, Who am I as a _____? (pastor, chaplain, educator, etc.). The professional minister is also discovering Christian people who don't treat others well. If professional ministers can survive this period of disillusionment, they are likely to stay in professional ministry. If this early stage is too overwhelming or discouraging, younger professional ministers may explore other options and return to school to retrain for a new career. Middle-aged ministers who are new to professional ministry will be more likely to return to the career they practiced before entering seminary than to explore further career options.

Early Career Development Issues

For those who integrate the disillusionment with other ambiguities of life within the first five years, questions of commitment then become central. How committed do I want to be to this denomination? this church? Some professional ministers choose to be deeply involved in denominational life, while others say with Tevye from *Fiddler on the Roof,* "God bless the Czar and keep him far from us!"

Questions about the importance of climbing the ladder to a "bigger" position eventually must be addressed. Many of these questions are about preferred role, setting, and geographic location.

This is also the stage at which professional ministers begin asking questions about values and advancement. In what setting of professional ministry can I work and not compromise my values? The values may be about establishing a satisfying personal life, family life, work ethic, and more.

As you can see, the developmental stage of early career is a busy time. Besides the issues addressed above, one's identity, competency, alliances, and advancement are also concerns during this pivotal time.

If you have been working in professional ministry for five years or less, use these pages to reflect on the following issues:

A. I have these thoughts and feelings about my identity and competence as a professional minister.

What actions do I need to take now to be the author of my own career development rather than let someone else write my career script?

B. I have the following thoughts and feelings about commitment to my denomination.

What actions do I need to take now to remain active in my own career development regarding my denomination?

C. Is forming relationships with peers a priority to me at this stage of my career development?

What actions do I need to take now to have the kind of relationship I choose with ministerial peers?

D. In early career, what resolution have I negotiated concerning the conflict between ministry and family and my role in my family's life?

What actions do I need to take now to have the type of family relationship that I want?

Mid-Career Developmental Issues

The developmental task of mid-career is reevaluation. Do I want to keep working so hard? How do I reenter the family after years of working late hours and every weekend? After the children are grown, what will my role in the family be? How do I continue feeling that I am a contributor to my professional ministry even though I likely will have no more advancements?

For the mid-career professional minister the question is no longer, "Who am I?" Ministry skills have been developed and honed for the past 20 or more years. Now the question becomes "Who am I as a minister in terms of age and years of experience?" Skills are no longer the issue; the meaning of my work is.

Commitment also becomes more about meaning and less about how near or far one wants to be in relation to the "bureaucracy" of one's denomination. Often in the mid-career developmental stage, concern about advancement takes a back seat to concerns about making a lasting contribution and passing the professional ministry on to the next generation. Mid-career is the time when many professional ministers see younger clergy getting the bigger appointments. Making peace with the career position one has reached is a mid-career task as well.

Family issues take on new meaning and possibilities. After spending many evenings away from the family launching one's career, it is now time to reenter the family. Often this reentry is poorly timed, since the family may be realigning because of graduations, geographical moves, aging parents, or changing relationships with significant others. If married, the minister will need to renegotiate roles with the spouse.

If you are in mid-career, use these pages to reflect about:

A. Currently, what are my concerns and satisfactions about my identity and competence?

    What actions do I need to take now to continue being an active participant in my own career development?

B. In mid-career, what am I thinking about how involved in denominational life I want to be?

    What actions do I need to take now to become involved in denominational life, to remain active in my denomination's life, or to become less involved than I am?

C. Does making a lasting contribution take precedence over climbing the career ladder in my mid-career development?

What actions do I need to take now to make a lasting contribution and/or continue moving up in my career?

D. In mid-career, are my relationships with peers and friends becoming of higher importance, lower importance, or of equal importance to me?

What actions do I need to take now to remain involved with ministerial peers?

E. In mid-career, what resolution have I negotiated concerning the conflict between ministry and family and my role in my family's life?

What actions do I need to take now to remain physically and emotionally connected to my family?

Late-Career Developmental Issues

In late career, competency and identity issues move to a new level. You are now one of the older pastors in your diocese, association, or conference. At this developmental stage one also asks, "How might I leave a legacy that will symbolize my contributions and live on after I am gone? Clergy have achieved this legacy in many ways, from mentoring younger clergy to having a building named after them.

Coming to terms with one's contributions is another important developmental process for the late-career professional minister. Along with coming to terms with one's career, one needs to find sources of commitment and involvement outside the current ministry setting. It is important for you, the late-career pastor, to "let go" of a congregation at retirement. It is equally important for the pastor who follows you. Consider the horror story we all know of the retired pastor who kept his secretary and an office at the church!

This developmental phase will naturally usher in grief. At retirement, for example, relationships will change: One won't be seeing the same parishioners and colleagues each day or every week. Depending on your denomination and if you serve as a parish pastor, there may be formal or informal guidelines about how much contact (and under what circumstances) you can have with the former church and church members.

Issues surrounding work and family also take a developmental turn. For many retired clergy, one's spouse, children, and outside activities are enough. Many, however, continue some level of activity with churches. This may range from occasional supply preaching to being an "intentional interim" to serving a church as part-time pastor.

If you are in late career, use these pages to reflect about:

A. Currently, what are my concerns and satisfactions about my identity and competence?

What actions do I need to take now to write the last chapter of my career?

B. In late career, this is what I am thinking about my commitment to my denomination.

What actions do I need to take now to leave a legacy to my denomination?

C. In late career does being a mentor takes precedence over climbing the career ladder for me?

What actions do I need to take now to remain active being a mentor to younger clergy?

D. In late career how much value am I placing on my relationships with peers?

What actions do I need to take now to remain connected to my peers and to make new relationships as my peers move off the scene?

E. In late career, what resolution have I negotiated concerning the conflict between ministry and family and my role in the life of my nuclear family and extended family?

What actions do I need to take now to stay connected to my family members?

Being aware of our current developmental stage in ministry, recognizing the natural tension that develops when one era overlaps another (for example, early career is ending, and middle career is beginning), and remembering that this is a normal process in which we take an active role—all these can make the stages of a ministerial career something to anticipate rather than fear.

Now let's turn to what we are likely to lose, what will stay the same, and what we will gain while making a career transition.

Loss during Career Change

The earliest significant loss I encountered that affected my career was the loss of my family when I was nine years old. I have spoken of this briefly in chapter 2. The loss was further heightened since my mother, grandmother, and I lived in Georgia after my parents' divorce, but my father moved to California. I literally lost my father emotionally and physically.

My mother went to work; my grandmother was at home with me, and life resumed a new kind of daily normality. By the time I was 13, Nanny, my grandmother, had a disease that ultimately robbed her of the ability to stand or walk. She had to live the last two years of her life in a nursing home. Because of her absence, I started taking on more household duties and often visited Nanny at the nursing home. By the time I was an early teen-ager I was living in an adult world with adult responsibilities.

The bright place in my life during these years was church. At church I became a leader. I was youth pastor during youth week. I taught a class of boys in Sunday school when I was only a boy myself. I sang in a boys' quartet and the youth choir. I won an associational speaker's tournament. By the time I was 15 (the year my grandmother died), I had already determined that I wanted (and God had called me) to be a pastor. After high school and college I went to seminary, earning both a master's degree in ministry and a doctoral degree in psychology and counseling.

One year after completing my doctoral degree I embarked on a fast track to become a leader in my denomination, only to discover that my denomination was getting a divorce, just as my parents had divorced years earlier. The split resulted from a systematic takeover of the Southern Baptist Convention by the fundamentalist wing of the denomination. The faction began its takeover in 1979 and had completed it by the mid-1980s, by which time fundamentalists held a majority of seats on the trustee boards of all SBC agencies. The breakup was couched in theological terms, but it was (and is) a divorce nonetheless. One could say the moderates moved to Georgia; the fundamentalists moved to California. I lost my family again.

Emotionally, I felt abandoned once more. I reacted by becoming depressed. The loss of my denominational family paralleled the loss of my family of origin. I do not know how much the depression was actually a matter of grieving again the earlier loss, although I suspect a great deal of it was. I do know that the two experiences felt alike. There was one significant difference. As a child of divorced parents, I was largely helpless to change my circumstances. As an adult from a divorced denomination, I could reinvent myself.

I did not stay stuck in the losses of my denomination. I left my denominational position—not because I had to but because I could not stay with any sense of integrity. I believe I felt the loss as keenly as if I had been fired. Yet I was determined to write a positive story about my response to the loss. So I left denominational life and went to an even better (according to many) position. I became the minister of pastoral care in a large, prestigious congregation.

What I had not counted on was how this loss would affect my entire family and all the social systems I touched and was touched by in a meaningful way. Their story is not mine to tell. However, the loss of our city, friends, schools, workplace, and the security that comes with knowing and liking our place in that locale and with those people was disturbing. My story is mine to tell, so that is where I will start.

Whenever we lose a job, whether voluntarily or by force, the natural tendency is to say, "This is about me; it is my fault." What is much harder to see is how the workplace (for most clergy, it will be the parish) was a central factor in our identity. Perhaps the place from which you lost your job and career identity was a closed system, so the new ideas you brought in felt threatening to others in the system. You may have been called to this church because "we need new blood," only to be told a year later that you were too young to be the minister! You may have attempted to infuse too many new ideas into the church and overwhelmed or frightened the people in the pews. Maybe the system used scapegoats to avoid responsibility for their internal problems, and you were the most obvious scapegoat. I have a friend who calls this phenomenon the reciprocal process. It means that losing your job is not only about you but also about the institution (church, school) that called you. Both of us—the institution and the employee—play a role in the job loss.

I also found myself becoming an expert at beating myself up mentally. I had friends who stayed in denominational ministry who believed they could do their work without compromising themselves. If they could do that, why couldn't I? I must have beat myself over the head with that question a thousand times. Even though I chose to leave, my insides felt as though I had done something wrong. If only I had been more resilient or adaptable or subversive or—I could have stayed.

Not only had my career within the denomination advanced, but my wife's career in education had. By the time I left my denominational job, she was dean in a local school. My wife was brave during the transition, saying she knew we all would make the transition well. Looking back, I think she was too brave. She was fortunate enough to land a job as department head in a private school in our new city. Our children were both enrolled in excellent schools, and people seemed helpful and friendly. So far, so good.

Within the first three months, however, we became aware that the new community was very different from what we were used to. The major employers in the community were the military and NASA. The area was dominated by soft money and bureaucracy. A level of paranoia pervaded the town, because the constant threat of federal cuts in defense and space spending hovered over the local residents as humidity shrouds New Orleans on an August afternoon. The folk brought all these community attitudes to church with them.

We underestimated our grief over leaving the old system. The grief was so gripping it both marked and marred our early days in the new jobs. It is difficult to work effectively while grieving deeply. I dealt with my grief by working 15-hour days, six days a week. It was my way of attempting to heal the gaping wound in my psyche and to anesthetize the pain. I'd gone from working for the national church in all 50 states to one city block, and the shrinking platform hurt.

Slowly, the pain did subside, so that within two years after the transition began we had a new life that was predictable, though not as satisfying as the old life.

LEARNING FROM OTHERS

Clergy have a unique vantage point from which to view individuals and their families as they navigate career storms. One can learn from parishioners who have made a transition well. Take Pat and John as an example. They had moved to New Orleans one year earlier than we had because the oil business was on the rise again. John had been offered a job plus benefits with a young maverick oil company that sounded too good to be true for the range of salary a geologist should be offered. After being with the company for several months, he discovered the package was indeed too good to be true. Within a year, oil prices had gone down, and John was unemployed.

I watched Pat and John with a sense of awe as they allowed this crisis to pull them together. No fault was assigned; the job loss was a historical event that simply happened. John explored new career options freely. Pat supported John through his "This is my fault" phase without assigning blame.

In the end John chose to reinvent himself in a moderate manner. He began exploring job possibilities in his chosen field, successfully landing three offers. John chose an offer with a large, reputable oil firm. It wasn't as much income as he'd had in the maverick company, but he traded higher pay for more security.

Pat and John's marital relationship was strengthened during the crisis as they developed a plan and followed it. Often the stress of career upheavals can cause marital upheavals also. How a couple handles that time is a choice based on many factors, such as old hurts not yet healed, each person's level of maturity, and how much self-centeredness is in the partners. Other factors include how much skill each person has in communicating, self-differentiating, and even in imagining alternatives. The opportunity to learn from church members who navigate crises creatively and flexibly is one of the good gifts of being in ministry.

Losing a job either by force or by choice affects you and your family. It will probably also affect the parish. Janie had been a Christian educator since seminary graduation. She began in a small, affluent parish that valued ministers and expected them to build a relationship with their parishioners. In fact, this relational style, coupled with high-quality work as a Christian educator, is what Janie had to offer. Janie thrived in that culture.

Janie served that parish five years before moving to a much larger congregation that emphasized making available many programs for all ages. Janie had no time for relationships, and by the end of the day found herself either too angry to sleep or crying herself to sleep.

It has been ten days since Janie resigned without another position arranged, although she is thinking about entering one of the other helping professions. The office atmosphere feels as if a death has occurred. At the end of this week, Janie is leaving. Many staff members now feel exposed and vulnerable in ways they hadn't when they knew Janie would be there, because they had come to rely on her strong sense of presence and competency. Relationships between Janie and the church staff, both administrative and professional, have begun to change. Janie's administrative assistant cannot look at her without having to dab tears from her eyes. The senior pastor is looking past her, as if she had already left her position with the church. A few colleagues tell her they wish they had the courage to do what she's done. Most express their regrets that she is leaving, and then go on with their work.

Janie is also surprised by her own reactions. She is pleased to be leaving this parish. She is confident of her future, even though the path is not clear. But she also finds herself feeling guilty. She was telling a wise friend about this unusual reaction. The friend told her that combat soldiers feel guilty after they survive and a buddy does not. This response is called survivor's guilt. Being able to name the feeling is helping Janie put this issue in perspective. She is seeing that she can care about folk with whom she worked without having to be responsible for their lives or changing the culture of a parish.

Janie has had a small but close-knit group of friends within the church. Several of them have already taken her out to dinner, heard her story about why she resigned, and supported her decision. Others have surprised her with almost the reverse reaction. Mainly they have avoided her. When she and one of her group ended in a room today alone, the church member began fussing at her about deciding to leave the church. After the confrontation, Janie was confused by her friend's anger toward her.

QUESTIONS FOR REFLECTION

1. List below the persons or groups you have lost or potentially might lose as you reinvent yourself.

2. Who or which of these is it important to leave behind to move on with your life and career? (An example is an abusive supervisor or someone who is overcontrolling.)

3. Which people and groups is it important for you to keep intact, if possible? Why?

4. What strategies can help you minimize the loss?

When you leave your job in a system, the whole system is affected, not just you. Reinventing yourself vocationally will affect every system you are meaningfully involved with—the work environment you are leaving, your spouse, and your children. Job loss is reciprocal in nature. It is not only about you—your job loss says something about the parish or institution you worked in.

When you lose your place in a work system by choice or fate, it will affect you, the system, your family, and all other systems that are meaningful to you.

Fortunately, life calls us forward.

SOME THINGS STAY THE SAME DURING TRANSITION

It is important to keep any loss in perspective. It is easy to say to yourself, "I've lost everything." What would be more accurate is to say, "I've lost my job." No doubt saying "I've lost everything" is an expression of what the loss feels like on the inside, rather than the reality of the loss.

Because of this tendency to see career change as catastrophic, it is also important to choose how you talk to yourself. Whenever your "self-talk" characterizes the loss as pervasive ("This has ruined all of my life!") or permanent ("I'll never be able to reinvent my life"), new self-talk is called for. More helpful responses might include, "Thank God this is only one area of my life," or "In time I'll be in a better-fitting job and work culture. I'm impatient, but it's worth the wait!"

A new field of marriage and family therapy is called narrative therapy. It emphasizes the fact that we are all writing a story about our lives. Some people's stories may read as if they are victims. Other people may write their stories as if they are responsible individuals able to act on behalf of themselves, even in transition times.

You are the author of how you think about yourself and what you say when you talk to yourself. The story you write about yourself is most likely how your life story will unfold. If you find yourself persistently writing a self-destructive or negative story about yourself, I would encourage you to seek out a pastoral counselor for help.

Another system I've kept with me has been my family. You may remember the Gospel story when Jesus' mother and brothers are standing outside a house waiting to see him. Someone lets Jesus know they are there, to which Jesus responds, "Who is my mother and who is my brother?" (Matthew 12:45ff., CEV). Then Jesus goes on to say his true kindred are those who do God's will.

Your family will also stay the same. Some of these people are kindred by blood; others are kindred spirits. Sometimes blood kin freeze their image of you at a certain age and have a difficult time seeing that you have grown past that age. When that happens, family is rarely able to see you as big enough or strong enough to reinvent yourself.

I know a woman who as an adult decided to go to medical school. She and her family believed she could reinvent herself as a family doctor, and she did so very successfully. She wrote a new chapter to her story that included medicine, and her family helped her write this new chapter.

If your family of origin can free you and bless you to be whatever you want to be, stay close to them. If they cannot, then take Jesus' advice and find brothers, sisters, mothers, and fathers who can. To continue returning to a poisoned well is a dangerous habit. Grieve the loss, and find "family" that is health-giving.

Marriage merits special attention in any transition time. You may be astounded that the person with the most resistance to your making a change is your spouse. Be cautious in interpreting your spouse's responses to your career transition. A story that begins, "My husband is afraid of change" is very different from one that opens, "She has always tried to hold me back!" The actions of spouses may mean they are scared, not that they don't want you to be happy.

I have also kept my close friends. These are people like Bruce, who was the best man at my wedding. We still talk at least once a month, even though we were in seminary together more than 25 years ago. My friends include people like Martin, who has not lost the art of letter writing. I think also of people like Dan, who inspires me to writing projects I'd not undertake without his encouragement.

I have only one handful of friends, but they are very important to me. My wife would tell you I work very hard to stay connected to them. She's right! The reason I do work hard at staying connected is that, with all the changes I have experienced in my life, they are a constant stabilizing force. These friends make me glad I am both alive and connected.

Through my career transition my professional peers have remained stable. These are people with whom I have always related only on a professional basis, yet they are trusted and valued colleagues.

While I was reinventing myself professionally, these people helped me in several valued ways. The first was that they gave me feedback I could trust. I can float an idea by these folk and expect honest feedback. These are the people who will say, "That idea will never work, but keep thinking," or "That's a great idea—can I help?"

A second way this network of professional peers helped me was to introduce me to others who could make my transition easier. When a peer is willing to open doors for you, a mature response is to say "Thank you" and walk through. Teenagers often do not want their parents' help. When one gets beyond adolescence, anyone who is willing and able to make life easier is most often seen as a person of blessing.

This system of professional peers has helped me understand cultures I am not familiar with so that I could broaden my job search beyond familiar terrain. I am grateful to an editor who showed me how to write a book proposal to submit to a publishing house. I would have never asked, "Are there any books similar to this in print?" I would not have shown in the proposal how I planned to help market the book. That editor did me a valuable service, for which I am still grateful to her.

QUESTIONS FOR REFLECTION

1. What social systems will remain the same during this time of reinventing yourself?

2. How do you feel about each group that will remain the same? And why do you feel that way?

SOME THINGS GET BETTER

After writing a first draft of this section, I realized I'd moved straight to the organizational piece without answering the question, "In reinventing myself, what and whom have I gained?" For me, in the midst of the transition, it was often difficult to see what I might gain or even have already gained. Yet gains are present. After reflecting, I recognize five in my story. You'll have gains also; be alert to see them.

I have gained new denominational connections. I have become a regular participant in the local clergy meeting of the United Church of Christ. Over time, I have come to know some of these people on more than a superficial level. They help me feel connected to my new denomination.

I have also made new denominational connections by serving as a member of the associational church and ministry committee. This committee meets with people seeking an official ministerial relationship with the United Church of Christ. It has been a fast-track learning experience! It has also given me a small group with which to be involved about denominational issues.

Through professional reinvention I have also gained new professional colleagues. I have gained colleagues both in the new denomination I've joined and in the institute where I teach and serve as an administrator.

I have also regained a town. Nearly 25 years ago my wife and I moved to New Orleans so that I could begin doctoral study. After we'd each earned a degree and had our first child, we moved. For the next 18 years we visited New Orleans as often as possible because we missed the city. By reinventing myself as a counselor-educator, I put myself in a position that allowed me to regain a city I love!

There is a final gain I have experienced. It is a more mature relationship with my wife. Somehow, coming through all our experiences together has made us stronger and more solid as a couple. Even though I am not fully sure how to describe this gain, I know it is real.

The 1980s movie *Back to the Future* would be an appropriate heading for this section. The new system you are entering (or have entered) is as intent on preserving itself as the old system you left. A system's first (and last) instinct is preservation. On the other hand, you are going to the future. The future is where hope resides. It is the belief that I can successfully reinvent myself to be a professional person more of my choosing in a more desired setting. Living in this tension that all systems are self-preserving (so don't be too naïve) and that the future is where hope resides (so don't be too pessimistic) is the trick to moving successfully into a new system. Listed below are five important lessons I have learned while going through career transition.

You cannot save this new system. Often people choose to reinvent themselves as a savior. Perhaps you have heard of someone having a helpful experience in counseling, so they decide to become a counselor. Sometimes those folk are disappointed because they are not able to be as helpful as they had hoped to be. Lawyers, doctors, ministers can all tell their stories of disappointments.

Remember, you cannot save the new system. The new system will not save me, either! People who successfully reinvent themselves do so for complex reasons, such as their desire for fulfillment and to contribute to the next generation. One Savior is all we need.

Remember, the new system will not save you. I have learned to be careful what I pick from the information grapevine of the workplace. Every system has a grapevine— and the grapes are most often rotten! Take care in how many grapes you ingest, because they will affect your well-being in the organization.

My most recent reinvention of myself (since completing my formal education, I've been through three reinventions) is as director of a pastoral-counselor education program. I continue to be astonished as I hear bits and pieces from the grapevine. What is even more astonishing is that I have kept a tally of accuracy for six months, and the accuracy rate is 0 percent! Every rumor has been false! Eat from the grapevine at your own risk!

Remember, whining is not a leadership quality. Every system has a whine factor, so be careful how deeply you drink. I know it is a play on words, but you get the message. Whining is intoxicating, whether you are 18 months old or have spent 18 years in the same career. Whining keeps you a victim. To be an actor in the affairs of your life, stop whining. Whining is bad for your health spiritually, physically, and emotionally.

Remember, view the new system as a whole. It is likely that you found good and bad in the old system you left. Now you have reinvented yourself in a new career, and guess what? You will find some good and some bad in the new system also. Viewing it holistically is the key. Looking only at the bad will depress you, perhaps even immobilize you. Seeing only the good will keep you naïve and vulnerable. Seeing your new system as it is, with some good and some bad, will help you stay both genuinely hopeful and safe as you move into this new world you are creating for yourself.

When you reinvent yourself, you are going back to the future. You are going back because the place you have created will be more similar to the old than dissimilar. You'll also be going to the future, where hope resides as you reinvent yourself.

Chapter 1. The Original Vision of Our Call

1. Nelle Morton, *A Leader's Guide to The Journey Is Home* (Louisville: Presbyterian Church [USA], 1989), 1.

2. Paul Tillich, *The Shaking of the Foundation* (New York: Charles Scribner's Sons, 1948), 162.

3. Frederick Buechner, *The Longing for Home* (San Francisco: HarperCollins, 1996), 7-8.

4. D. H. Lawrence, *Apocalypse* (London: Penguin, 1995), 92.

5. Thomas Moore, *Care of the Soul* (San Francisco: HarperCollins, 1992), 243-244.

6. James Hillman, *The Soul's Code* (New York: Random House, 1996), 3.

7. Annie Dillard, *The Annie Dillard Reader* (New York: Harper Perennial, 1994), 126.

8. C. G. Jung, *The Development of Personality*, collected works, vol. 17 (New York: Princeton University Press, 1954), 175-176.

9. Buechner, *Wishful Thinking* (New York: Harper & Row, 1973), 95.

Chapter 2. Exploring God's Call

1. H. Richard Niebuhr, Daniel Day Williams, and James M. Gustafson, *The Purpose of the Church and Its Ministry* (New York: Harper & Brother, 1956).

2. Margaret Guenther, *Holy Listening* (Cambridge, Mass.: Cowley Publications, 1992).

3. Jeffrey L. Zimmerman and Victoria C. Dickerson, *If Problems Talked: Narrative Therapy in Action* (New York: Guilford Press), 4.

Chapter 3. Managing Anxiety in Times of Change

1. Margaret Wheatley, "The Unplanned Organization," *Noetic Sciences Review* 37 (Spring 1996): 23.

2. Michael Kerr and Murray Bowen, *Family Evaluation* (New York: W. W. Norton, 1988), 112.

3. *The Barnhart Concise Dictionary of Etymology*, Robert K. Barnhart, ed. (New York: HarperCollins, 1995), 30.

4. Edwin H. Friedman, *Friedman's Fables* (New York: Guilford Press, 1990), 9.

5. Edwin Friedman, Minister's Week lecture (Dallas: Southern Methodist University, 1996).

6. T. S. Eliot, "East Coker," from *The Complete Poems and Plays* (New York: Harcourt Brace, 1980), 126-127.

Chapter 4. Surviving the Change

1. Rodney Hunter, gen. ed., *Dictionary of Pastoral Care and Counseling* (Nashville: Abingdon, 1990), 576.

2. Joseph Fabry, *Guideposts to Meaning: Discovering What Really Matters* (Oakland: New Harbinger Publications, 1988.), 94-97.

$\mathcal{W}$elcome to the work of Alban Institute...
the leading publisher and congregational
resource organization for clergy and laity today.

Your purchase of this book means you have an interest in the kinds of information, research, consulting, networking opportunities and educational seminars that Alban Institute produces and provides. We are a non-denominational, non-profit 25-year-old membership organization dedicated to providing practical and useful support to religious congregations and those who participate in and lead them.

Alban is acknowledged as a pioneer in learning and teaching on *Conflict Management *Faith and Money *Congregational Growth and Change *Leadership Development *Mission and Planning *Clergy Recruitment and Training *Clergy Support, Self-Care and Transition *Spirituality and Faith Development *Congregational Security.

Our membership is comprised of over 8,000 clergy, lay leaders, congregations and institutions who benefit from:
- ❖ 15% discount on hundreds of Alban books
- ❖ $50 per-course tuition discount on education seminars
- ❖ Subscription to *Congregations*, the Alban journal (a $30 value)
- ❖ Access to Alban research and (soon) the "Members-Only" archival section of our web site www.alban.org

For more information on Alban membership or to be added to our catalog mailing list, call 1-800-486-1318, ext.243 or return this form.

Name and Title: _____

Congregation/Organization: _____

Address: _____

City: _____ Tel.: _____

State: _____ Zip: _____ Email: _____

BKIN

The Alban Institute
Attn: Membership Dept.
7315 Wisconsin Avenue
Suite 1250 West
Bethesda, MD 20814--3211